NETWORK
YOUR WAY TO
MILLIONS

The Definitive Step-by-Step Guide
to Wealth Through Network Marketing

BY RUSS PALEY

To order additional copies, call:

1-800-BOOK-LOG
or
1-800-266-5564

Published by Wealth Building Publications, Inc.
4984 Boxwood Circle
Boynton Beach, Florida 33436

This publication is designed to provide accurate and authoritative information in regard to the subject matter covered. It is sold with the understanding that the publisher is not engaged in rendering legal or accounting services. If legal advice or other expert assistance is required, the services of a competent professional should be sought.

From a Declaration of Principles by an Association and a Committee of Publishers and Associations.

ISBN 0-9672238-0-6

Credits and Contacts

Author: Russ Paley
RPnetwking@aol.com
Editing and interior design: Walt Kleine, Kleine Editorial Services
wkleine@netwiz.net
Graphics: Adi Kessler
adigrfx@aol.com
Cartoons: Andrew Toos, Toos Studios
Drewtoos@aol.com
Cover design: Suzanne Hassler
Suzhassler@aol.com
Photographer: Evan Auster
nave417@aol.com
Marketing: Joel Levin
mediajoel@aol.com

TABLE OF CONTENTS

This book is invaluable for anyone who is thinking about joining a networking opportunity. *Network Your Way to Millions* is also a great step-by-step plan for those already involved in a network marketing business. It literally covers everything a networker needs to make millions.

—VENUS ANDRECHT
Author of *MLM Magic*

"Only 4½ years ago, I was working 70 hours a week for a corporation and barely getting by. With the skills and step-by-step strategies I learned from Russ, I went from zero experience to a very strong six-figure residual income."

—DANIEL TORE, NJ

"The key elements in my success are the guidance and brilliant strategies of Russell Paley. He helped me earn five figures a month part-time in my first full year in my business, something I was not able to do in 15 years of network marketing."

—PAUL KUPETSKY, NY
"The Midas Muffler man"

"Why re-invent the wheel? Don't waste your time and grope in the dark when you can easily follow the leader. Russ has made it to the top and can show you how to get there, too. Network Your Way is not only inspirational, but also written so you can use the principles *immediately* to create your own mega-success story."

—DEBORAH HALPERIN PONEMAN
Founder and CEO, YES TO SUCCESS
Contributor to *Chicken Soup for the Soul*

"In the near future, almost everyone in America will be participating in network marketing as sellers and/or consumers. The people who create wealth for themselves will most likely be those who have read Russ Paley's book and are implementing its powerfully-effective strategies."

—JOE TYE, author of *Never Fear; Never Quit*

ABOUT THE AUTHOR

Russell Paley, celebrated for his financial triumphs in the home-based business industry, is also a nationally-known consultant, trainer, mentor and author. He has spoken about his no-nonsense methods of making it big without "going to work" each day before audiences on three continents.

Now 30, Russ started a business eight years ago, literally from a corner of his kitchen table. He has made over four million dollars in his self-employed years. He has discovered (and written this book about) the secrets of getting paid now for work done in the past. Each of the last two years has brought him in excess of one million dollars, almost all of it in automatic income.

Through Russ's mentoring and training, several thousand individuals and couples are making substantial part-time income and several hundred are making spectacular full-time income. In addition, he has trained hundreds of thousands of people through seminars, and millions more through satellite TV, audio tapes, videos and books.

The recipient of fifty-eight business awards and honors, Russ was named to the Outstanding Young Men of America last year. It was apparent he was destined for success when he was the top finance graduate of the Bryant Business School of Smithfield, Rhode Island, and was the winner of the prestigious Wall Street Journal Award.

Russ has homes in a New York suburb and on a Florida beachfront, and a vacation place in Arizona. He enjoys travel, outdoor sports, boating, and collecting sports memorabilia.

He says, "I can afford to retire now, but I'm having too much fun!"

CHAPTER ONE

INTRODUCTION
MY STORY

It was like a dream, being on television for the first time. A forty-five-minute make-up session, bright lights, cables snaking everywhere, frantic assistants consulting clipboards, the director gesturing.

There I was, standing in a big ballroom in front of several hundred men and women of all ages, with three TV cameras focused on my face. The audience was clapping wildly. They got to their feet and gave me a standing ovation for over a minute, as if I had just won an Oscar or Grammy.

I had just been introduced by the emcee, who compared me to the guy who broke the four-minute mile, the first man to reach the moon, or the first man to reach the summit of Mt. Everest. What an awesome feeling to be compared to Roger Bannister, Neil Armstrong, and Sir Edmund Hillary!

People watching me on monitors in other meeting places all over the world were also giving me a standing ovation. They must have believed I had just walked on water.

In reality, they were clapping and cheering because I had just been handed a check for $223,000, right there on the stage of a famous hotel. I had earned almost a quarter of a million dollars in just one month! I had smashed every record on the books of the company I represent–and this was in a new business I had started only recently. As they cheered, I was thinking, "I'm not a hero. I'm just an average guy who chose the right business."

I didn't need their applause. Believe me, the money was enough recognition! After all, I was newly rich and it had only been four years since I quit my regular job–much to the amusement of family and friends, and against their well-meaning advice.

That check, in December, 1995, was a small bump in my road to the millions I have made in my own home-based business.

Those tens of thousands of people cheering, all around the world, were mostly people I'd trained to do the same business that made me wealthy. They were cheering because they were happy for me, of course, but they were cheering more because they were happy for themselves and their own new success. They were cheering themselves as much as they cheered me, because they were on the winning team. Each individual was successful. No one was competing with anyone else. Can you think of a better win-win situation, or a better reason to cheer?

And my Aunt Ethel and Uncle Harry? My rich uncle in California? And Linda and Allen and Simon? Well...I'm not gloating about my prosperity, but I couldn't help recalling that they were the ones who told me I was crazy to leave the "security" of a big corporation. I put quotation marks around security because last year my former employer laid off 28,000 employees!

Think about that! *Twenty-eight thousand* people without jobs! *Twenty-eight thousand* people without income! Now you understand why personal bankruptcies are at an all-time high!

Escaping the Employee Trap

You're about to read a guide to how you can escape the traps and slow advancement of employment by someone else, over whom you have no control. After all, why does *anyone* work? Your goal should not be to make someone else rich. Your goal should be to do your financial best for yourself!

If you follow my suggestions in the following chapters, it's possible you'll be earning more in *one month* than you used to make in *one year*.

I'm offering to teach you how to run a business from your home, so you can become one of the smart ones; so you can become one of the wealthy ones–not one of those desperately seeking re-employment or desperately striving to move up some corporate ladder, if not desperately seeking to merely remain employed.

It does not hurt me in any way to share my ideas. In fact, it makes me feel very good inside. There's more than enough money to be made for you, *and* for me. And no, this is *not* too good to be true–unless you just sit there and do nothing with the knowledge I will share with you. Doing nothing makes no one wealthy.

These wealth-creating and wealth-building methods are real. They work. Just check out the testimonials in this book.

I'm an ordinary person with no special preparation for starting a business, but I've made millions. Many more millions of dollars have been made by other equally ordinary people who have followed my lead. I know how much has been made because some of them are "my people," whom I've trained, and who have followed my lead. Extraordinary people with high motivation have earned even more. Whichever type you are, I stake my reputation as a well-known trainer when I say, "*You* can make millions." This is not an exaggeration. All you have to do is read, listen, learn–and go do it!

How Did I Get Here?

My first employment out of college was a desk job at the national headquarters of a huge corporation. I was well-compensated, but I observed that the consultants who advised the company and the people who sold products to the company were making far more than I. Some didn't even "go to work" as I did. They worked out of their homes.

That sounded like a pretty good deal to me. If others could have a lifestyle of freedom and big money *working from home*, then I wanted that freedom and lifestyle, too. I wanted that corporate office to become ancient history in my life. I saw no reason why I could not enjoy a lifestyle of plenty of money and plenty of time.

That was my dream: time to enjoy the money and money to enjoy the time. That was what got me interested in a business with a home office as an alternative to living and working within the confines of a corporate structure.

It is not necessary to quit your regular job instantly, financially cold turkey, to work from home. You can ease into working from home, developing your new business, while remaining with your employer until your new business has grown and is established.

Now, *this is important*. While I investigated various home business opportunities, I had the chance to see the best and worst of them. I examined opportunities from franchises to network marketing. I met both the originators of these businesses and the "little people" who ran the businesses from their homes.

The funny thing about the little people, though, is that some of them were raking in really big bucks, really big time! In many cases, the folks working out of their bedrooms or kitchens were making more money than the top executives in their parent companies!

Can you guess the rest of the story? It should be easy. I became one of those "little people" who would make the big bucks. I started working my new business in my spare time, from my home, and found myself growing rich. Now I am paid an *automatic income* every month, *based on work I did months ago*. These payments, according to my contract with my parent company, *will never end!*

Yes, it does feel unreal–but my bank account and investment portfolio don't lie. Neither do many months with a six-figure income–from a part-time job! And my Mercedes 500SL is not a mirage.

All this–and I have plenty of time to travel! And I travel first class! I can play sports, see friends and family, and really enjoy life. I have time to make money while in the middle of my swimming pool, using a cordless phone from a raft! (No, you don't want to get your phone wet!)

All this is true.

It all happened because I plugged into the right industry–and went out and *did it.*

Well, that's *my* story.

It could also be *your* story, in whatever way you chose to make it yours. You see, *you* have the opportunity to duplicate what I and some of my friends have achieved. This can become *your* reality because you hold in your hands the book that reveals the secrets.

The choice is yours.

Will you continue as you are?

Or will you take the steps to use the secrets of this book to change your life?

There's a saying that, "If you continue to do things the way you always have, then your future results will always be the same." This is a bit less true today than it used to be. "Doing things the way you always have" may get you "downsized," or just plain and honestly laid off, no matter how good you are at doing "what you've always done."

Do you want that?

If so–that's your choice to make. It wasn't mine, and it's not what I want for you.

In this book I'll show you what things to change and how to change them in order to accumulate wealth. You see, merely changing, for the sake of making changes, guarantees *nothing.* To change your life and achieve wealth, you must make the *right* changes. That's what this book is about.

My knowledge and secrets are all in this book. Use it! It's your road map of the expressway to freedom from financial stress. It's your ticket out of the corporation. It's your ticket to creating wealth from your home.

CHAPTER TWO

YOU'RE THE BOSS: LUCRATIVE ALTERNATIVES TO THE CORPORATE RUT

Home-business marketing gives you all the benefits of being in business for yourself without the high investment and high risks and other downsides which are a part of starting a typical business.

The first *and most important* advantage for many of you is low start-up cost. An average home-based networking business costs from $30 to $500 to start up.

Compare that to franchises that average $75,000!

Start-up costs of businesses you start on your own average over $50,000, not including inventory, employees, and overhead.

Do you want to look into a partnership arrangement? You're still looking at high investment, limited control of the business, and other undesirable financial risks. What if the partner wants to split up with you, right when you think things are going well, or sees things differently than you? And that's without worrying about real horror stories, like the partner who takes your (the company's) money, which has been set aside to pay the taxes, but instead leaves the country with the cash, leaving you to fight it out with the IRS over the taxes you thought were paid!

Another advantage of home-based marketing is that you have no employees. There's no hiring, no firing, and no illegal activity like employees (or partners) stealing or embezzling from your business. There are no pension plans to set up, fund, and maintain. *There is no overhead.*

You don't have to pay your employee's salaries and other company overhead expenses whether your business is profitable or not. There is no bookkeeping. There are no accounts payable. There are no accounts receivable. You don't need a degree in accounting or a college or post-graduate education to be successful.

Accounts receivable are major risks for most businesses. Every large company loses millions each year from non-collections. In home-based network marketing, the company bills and collects from the customers you bring in. You have no paperwork. Paperwork is a hassle in all other businesses, but not home-based marketing. In other businesses, you need employees with many forms of expertise. In home-based network marketing you don't need expert employees or paperwork. You don't need any employees at all.

Owning your own home-based networking business has major tax benefits.

Always consult your tax professional on tax matters. Tax laws, and the interpretation of them, change from year to year, and sometimes more often. Every person's tax situation and needs are different.

The following general information was provided to me by Randy S. Fischel, a CPA I trained in network marketing.

Randy earns over $8,000 a month working part time in network marketing, while continuing to own and operate his CPA firm. *Appendix A*, at the end of this book, is an interview with Mr. Fischel about tax considerations for a small or home-based business like network marketing.

These are a few of the normal tax write-offs in a network marketing business. You can normally deduct the costs of the starter kit package and the product sampler kit, give-aways you offer as sample products, your telephone bill, auto expenses (actual expenses versus the standard IRS cents-per-mile rate), parking, tolls, travel and lodging. Meals and entertainment are fifty percent deductible. Your business training, opportunity presentations when you invite new guests to join the network marketing company, and convention expenses are normally deductible. You can usually deduct for business use of your home (I'll get into that a bit later), your home office furniture and business equipment, accounting and tax fees, postage, gifts and promotions.

Let's talk about your automobile. Your car payment (or lease payment) and your auto insurance, repairs, maintenance and gas, etc., can be deducted to the extent that the mileage was for business purposes. Say you drive your automobile 30,000 miles a year. If thirty percent (9,000) of those miles are business miles, for example because you are driving from meeting to meeting to meeting, then thirty percent of your insurance, your gas, your repairs, maintenance and payments can be deducted using certain formulas. You can deduct whatever percentage of your actual expenses is equal to your percentage of business use. Your tax professional will look at whether your actual expenses or the standard per-mile rate (currently 31.5 cents a mile) will give you a larger deduction. Normally, actual expenses will be a better deduction.

Let's talk about the business use of your home. You can deduct a percentage of the cost of your mortgage or rent. Your mortgage interest is always deductible under current tax law (and it's not likely Congress will mess with *that* deduction!) The deductible percentage of other home business expenses is the amount of the total square footage of the home or apartment that is used "exclusively for business." (The IRS can get sticky about that "exclusively for business" qualification; ask your tax professional how to assure that your deduction is legal according to the IRS. You don't want to get burned should you be targeted for one of those nasty IRS audits!) You can deduct your real estate taxes, water and sewer charges, insurance, utilities, heat, repairs, maintenance, landscaping, a visit by the exterminator and so on. Ask your tax professional what you should list, and ask him or her to make sure you didn't miss anything.

You can deduct for business furniture and equipment, business accounting and tax preparation fees, postage, and all marketing expenses. You can't deduct calls to Aunt Harriet–unless she's working in your network. Christmas cards to members of your network, even if they're relatives, can be deducted as marketing and promotional expenses. (This is another area where it pays to check with your tax professional to assure everything you claim is legal.)

As a simplified example, let's say your mortgage payment (including interest) is $2,000 a month and you use twenty percent of your house for your business. Your "exclusively for business" office space is twenty percent of your house. Thus, $400 a month can be deducted out of your $2,000 a month payment. Twenty percent of your real estate taxes, your water and sewer charges, your homeowner's insurance, your utilities, your heat, repairs and maintenance, your landscaping, your exterminator and so on, can be deducted. (Note: you can deduct one hundred percent of your real estate taxes in any case, but when you file a business return, the "business use" portion of your home will show that percentage of your real estate taxes as a business expense, which affects your business income while the balance is an ordinary deduction–yes, it gets complicated; that's why you must use a tax professional!) You *must* use an appointment book or diary as an expense log, and you *must* obtain receipts for every expenditure you deduct. (You are *not* in business to have problems with the IRS, so the advice of a good tax professional is worth every penny you pay him or her!)

Let's say your telephone bill is $1,200 a year and your auto expenses are $6,000. Meals and entertainment are $2,600. Fifty percent of the cost of your meals and entertainment for business purposes is deductible, so that's $1,300. Your house or apartment expenses are $24,000. That adds up to $32,500. Assuming twenty percent of that is business expense, your deductible amount, twenty percent of $32,500 is $6,500. Assuming you're in the 35% tax bracket, 35% times $6,500 yields a tax savings of $2275.

That's a *very* powerful tax write-off just for owning your own home-based business!

When do You Want to Retire?

Let's talk about other benefits. The average person has $78,000 in savings at age 60 as a retirement nest egg. More and more people are living longer, and the average life-span of Americans (and much of the world) increases every year. Retirement planning becomes more and more critical for everyone.

Most people under the age of 60 (who are not in home-based networking) have neither time freedom nor financial freedom. They might have one or the other, but they don't have both.

Networking works to create residual income. Its greatest benefit is that with residual income you can have both time freedom and financial freedom.

According to the Bureau of Labor Statistics, the average person works forty hours a week, forty-eight weeks a year, for forty-five years. 40 x 48 x 45 is 86,400 hours. That's how long the average person works in a lifetime.

Isn't it rather frightening to think that 86,400 hours of work will leave you with only $78,000 in retirement savings? *That's less than a dollar for every hour you worked!*

Social Security may or may not be here much longer, or may (more likely) be radically different than the program we know today. Even if Social Security survives in essentially its present form, at best it will give you no more than 40 percent of the lifestyle you're used to–if your *only* income is Social Security.

Even with a company pension plan (if you're lucky enough to have one) to supplement Social Security, you're not much better off. Walt Kleine, my editor for this book, who has near-top Social Security income and a pension equal to more than half his SS payment, tells me, "I suppose I could live on it if all I did was sit in an apartment and watch TV–until the TV died. Maybe I could make it if I lived in South Nowheresville and didn't drive anywhere. I don't want to live like that. If I'd made that much money when I was 20, everyone would have been impressed by what a wonderful job I had and how lucky I was to be so well-paid.

Yeah, Russ, tell people to plan, for Heaven's sake, and tell them to be real hard-nosed about making their plan work!"

Walt is still working at 67–and he's one of the lucky ones. He's doing what he loves ("I wouldn't stop writing if I won the lottery"), and his health has been good.

Home-based networking could have solved his financial problem, as it can solve yours in today's much more complex society.

In home-based networking, you're paid for many years based on a one-time effort. You are not living paycheck to paycheck. In home-based network marketing, you can have *both* time freedom *and* financial freedom.

If you're my age, retirement may seem a long way off; something you can worry about later.

Don't let yourself be sucked into the "I'll worry about it tomorrow" trap!

The time to plan for retirement is *now*, regardless of your age. It's easier when you're young, when you are most likely to fall into the "tomorrow trap", but it's never too late!

Money isn't everything, of course. The line about "money can't buy happiness" is so old I don't know where it came from, but it's true. Money *helps*, but it only helps in the things financial freedom can provide. It can be awfully hard to be happy if you *don't* have money. Ask Walt, ask the 80-year-olds I talk about below, and ask many others who have learned the importance of having enough money. But if all you have in your life is money, you don't have much of a life.

I believe your goal should be to have *both* a good life and the money you need to enjoy it and make it better; money to make your life safe and secure, and money to provide an equally secure and rewarding retirement–whenever *you* choose to retire.

Has anyone told you that you should "get a life" when your whole focus is on making enough money to pay this month's bills? If not, count yourself lucky–or know that you've planned well.

Home-based marketing is about planning well–and, more important, ***making your plan work.***

I've interviewed hundreds of people in their 80s. *Every one of them* said they wished that they'd spent more time with their family and friends and worked less overtime. But that posed a dilemma for them. If they worked all the time, they didn't have *time freedom*. They didn't have time to spend with family and friends. If they took time for family and friends, they didn't make enough money to pay the bills, much less to retire with some degree of comfort. They lacked *financial freedom*.

Yet, if you listen to these elderly people who wished they'd worked less and lived more, you get a powerful message about the need to make enough money and to plan well. You can't do that with an ordinary job.

Each of us has a certain number of years to live. I want all of you to make the most of every minute in every hour in every day of every year!

How can you do that? What's the answer? The answer, I believe, is home-based network marketing. Take a look at the advantages:

The key advantage is *duplication/leverage*.

Let me give you an analogy. Imagine a snowball that starts at the top of a mountain and rolls down the side of that mountain. Perhaps it's just one snowflake that gathers another snowflake, that gathers another, until it's a snowball and can start rolling. The snowball starts off small, but suddenly, because it's rolling on a hill, it gathers more and more snow and more and more speed. It gets larger and larger and rolls faster and faster and faster until it reaches the bottom. By then it's become an avalanche–which is what happens when a snowball becomes a monster.

You don't want to see monster avalanches on the ski slopes, but in networking *that's exactly what you're striving for–and that's what happens in home-based network marketing.*

You start your organization and train your people to duplicate your efforts, like the snowflake gathers more snowflakes. All of a sudden, like the snowflake-to-snowball-to-avalanche progression, your organization grows and grows and grows with your efforts and it's growing so fast and so large you've lost all control. But the beauty of network marketing is that you don't have to control it! The company whose products or services you market takes care of that! All you have to do is keep adding more "snowflakes" (people) to your organization!

To show you how this principle works, imagine what happens if a penny is doubled every day for thirty days. On the first day, that penny is worth one cent. On the second day it is worth two cents. The third day it is worth four, then eight, then 16, 32, 64 cents, and $1.28. On the thirty-first day that penny is worth more than an amazing ten million dollars! That's because doubling (duplicating) the penny every day is an example of geometric progression.

The same geometric progression, the same principle of duplication, is true when you duplicate your marketing efforts and the growth of your organization. Every time you double yourself, you're working toward massive duplication and profit.

Of course no real organization grows at the perfectly even rate of the example, but you have only to look the progression of my income–see *About the Author* at the front of this book–to see the power of duplication at work. I worked, and I continue to work, to find people who will duplicate my efforts.

Ideally, every person you add to your organization will work with the same level of dedication as you and I, but reality is that some will produce, others will do only the minimum, and some will sign up and drop out. That's the reality of human nature. You could rate people on a scale of zero to ten–zero being the person who signs up, does nothing, and drops out, while ten is someone who shares your dedication and works as hard as you or harder.

If you find *one person* who is a ten on that scale, you have it made.

Reality is that most people are not tens. There are a variety of reasons for this–motivation, available time, and so on. Ideally, you're a ten, but reality is that you may not be, or for various reasons cannot be a ten in the perfectionist sense I use the term. That is, a ten would be someone who succeeds as I have–and there's only one of me! *So far!!!* (Come on, people, I'd like some company up here!)

Yes, I want everyone who reads this book to achieve as I have, and more! If you surpass me, *more power to you!* The beauty of networking is that your success does not diminish mine, nor does my success diminish yours. We are helping each other succeed!

But I'm talking reality in this book. Reality is that most people in home-based networking or any other kind of business will not achieve my level of success–*which does not mean they don't succeed!* You, and they, like me, will achieve the level of success you want and can work for. Note that I said "can" work for. If you're working two jobs just to pay the rent, it's going to be harder to succeed–at anything–than if you have more free time to work at network marketing.

A two-jobs-to-pay-the-rent single mother, for example, or a multiple-job father of four, for another example, would need to make an extraordinary leap of faith to drop one of those jobs and devote his or her full time efforts to a network marketing opportunity until that networking opportunity has become profitable for that person–or has not.

Does this sound like I'm being negative? *Not in the least!*

I'm describing the second advantage of home-based network marketing, the unique, truly awesome advantage which makes it possible even for that single mother or father of many children with two jobs to succeed.

The second advantage is that you can do network marketing at your own pace!

You can make network marketing fit your personal needs, goals, lifestyle and available time!

It doesn't matter whether you're a ten, or whether you have a ten in your organization. *You can succeed.* If you work yourself up to being a five, say, you'll have people in your organization who are fours and fives, and better. If you're a four or five, you may well find a ten to bring into your organization! And the neat thing is that as you bring in people who rate higher on the scale, you'll find yourself rising up the scale, too! As the people you bring into your organization become productive, you, too, will be more productive! *Everything multiplies your work!* The more you do, the more it multiplies!

If you're that two-jobs-to-pay-the-rent person, you may wonder how you'll find time to bring even *one* person into your organization. But it's easy! You have two jobs, which means two sets of co-workers who know and trust you! Friends, family and co-workers are the first people you market to! If you present the opportunity well, they'll be glad they listened to you! Those who didn't sign up at your first presentation may sign up later, when they see your success, and the success of those who did sign up and work at the opportunity.

Now, let me offer the *power of one* theory. Suppose you duplicate your efforts and you find a ten. A ten is usually someone with marketing experience, a real go-getter. That ten will most likely will find another ten, who will find a ten, who will find a ten, and so on. When you find a ten, the chances are that person knows and will market to other tens! Now, if you have 10 x 10 x 10 x 10 working in your organization, you will have 10,000 hours of production because of duplication! Even if you're not a ten yourself, you may find a ten and have the benefit of tens working in your downline.

That's an example of how things can work when everything is perfect, but few of us and few things in life are perfect tens. It's more realistic, and a lot more common, for you to be, say, a five. If you find another five, who finds another five, who finds another five, the same principle applies–5 x 5 x 5 x 5 is 3,125 hours of duplication! That's a lot of real-world production–just because you found one five! That's the real, practical, every-day power of network marketing!

You pass on your knowledge to those who join your organization as the first layer in your downline. You teach your new partners everything you've learned and are practicing, especially techniques for creating their own downlines. (I'll talk about downlines later.) What you're doing is cloning yourself. You are cloning your own success, and helping your downline achieve success as you have. You are creating a major win-win situation.

This is the most basic technique of network marketing. Clone yourself! Clone your knowledge into others and earn residual income from their entire business!

There's a book called *The Six Degrees of Separation*. That book says that if you know six people, *you know everybody* because if you know six people, most likely one of those six people knows somebody you know, and one of those six people knows somebody that they know. In essence, you know everybody if you know six people. We are all connected, one way or another–and most of us know a lot more than seven people!

In home-based marketing, that "Six Degrees of Separation" principle is exceptionally powerful. Networking is a word-of-mouth business. (As I said above, the two-jobs-to-pay-the-rent person actually may have an unexpected advantage; he or she has two sets of co-workers–even *more* people who know more people!)

Just the simple fact that you know people whom you talk to, who talk to their friends, who talk to their friends, etc., makes word-of-mouth advertising the most powerful marketing tool there is–and it's ideal for network marketing. That's why ordinary people talking to other ordinary people can create remarkable success for themselves, each other, and everyone they know and contact.

Another key advantage of network marketing is that you make money on the orders of people you don't even know and have never met.

Suppose you, personally, train and bring into your organization one hundred people and, on average, they each work one hour a day. Someone who works one hour a day might rate a two or three, or at most a four on that zero-to-ten scale. But you have one hundred people in your business who are marketing your program one hour a day! All of a sudden you are paid on a hundred hours a day of production and output based on helping those one hundred people go out and do this as a business. That's powerful because you can't work one hundred hours a day at *any* job! There aren't that many hours in the day, even if you didn't need sleep, time for pleasure, and could keep going at full power the entire time! There just aren't that many hours in a day–the most you could work is eighteen hours, if you could survive on six hours sleep, and have no other life!

You see, while it's nice if you're a ten, and absolutely wonderful if you find a ten, you can achieve wonderful success with an organization of twos and threes!

The next benefit of network marketing is that *anybody can become successful*. Your age, sex, religious background, or previous experience doesn't matter! *You can succeed!*

Let me give you some examples of people I've enrolled.

Nadine enrolled when she was a twenty-year-old college student. She had no business experience. She's making a six-figure income at the age of twenty-five!

I enrolled Greg, an unemployed wire and cable telephone man who'd gone bankrupt. He and Sheri, his wife, are now making over $500,000 a year!

I've enrolled CPAs. I've enrolled cardiologists. I've enrolled successful multimillionaire business owners, and I've enrolled homemakers who are earning a great income.

Network marketing is the equalizer of all businesses.

All you need to do is to work hard on a part-time or full-time basis. That's what determines our success–hard work finding customers to call, who will order products directly from the network marketing company. I won't say that the number of hours you devote to network marketing is not important. Of course it is! The more hours you devote, the more success you can achieve. But, far more important than the number of hours is your dedication and how hard you work at it, even if you only have the one hour a day of my example, above. Even if you have *only one* hour a day, perhaps three days a week, when you work, *work hard*, with complete dedication.

That's the key to success!

Another of the biggest benefits of network marketing is that you can help other people make money in the process of making money yourself. You can change their lives forever as you change yours.

What a *great* concept!

The more you help your organization make money and help the people who work with you to make money, the more money you make! There is no cutthroat competition, like you often encounter when working in regular businesses. There is no jealousy because someone thinks, *"that* person is going to get a promotion and I'm not!"

Network marketing is not only a win-win concept; it can't work any other way!

Another advantage of network marketing is that *you are your own boss.* There's flexibility in that. You can make your own hours. Once you're doing network marketing full-time, there's no alarm clock going off in the morning–unless you choose to set it. *You can choose your own part-time hours. Most network marketing successes start part-time. Part-time network marketing income will supplement your regular-job income and let you be the best employee you can for the company that provides your paycheck–until you're ready to quit and devote full time to network marketing. When you do network marketing full time, you become the best entrepreneur you can be. You're no longer an employee, and you don't have employees!

When your network marketing income far exceeds the money you make on your regular job, you can make decisions on where and how far you want to go with this business. There is no red tape. There are no bureaucratic slowdowns. There's no corporate in-fighting. There are few restrictions. You can market and advertise almost anywhere. Your mind is free to imagine what you can do and market the way you want to without the restrictions that are built into other business endeavors.

Another advantage of network marketing is its unlimited income potential.

You don't have to wait for a raise or a promotion. *You create your own raise!* You're in control of your income!

Triangular Graph Showing A Corporate Pyramid

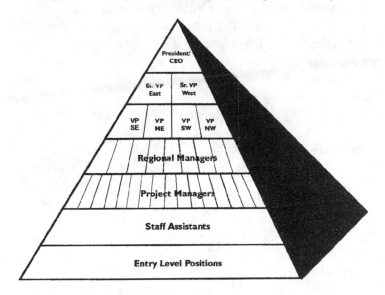

In most corporations, only a few people get to the top. Most employees are paid at the bottom of the corporate scale. There's room at the top for only a few positions that pay well–the CEO, CFO, VPs, department heads, and the top design and marketing people, etc.

In network marketing there is no risk of layoffs or "downsizing," that wonderful '80s and'90s corporate euphemism for "fired." You have security for the future.

Your success is totally in your hands if you go with a company that's over five years old. (I'll talk about the importance of how long a network marketing company has been in business later.) Great friendships are made because everyone is striving toward a common goal as a team.

I believe "team" stands for: *Together Everyone Achieves More*. You can work as much or as little as you want. You can take vacations when you want. The business will continue to provide you an income even when you're gone. That's because your income is *residual income*.

Residual income is one of the biggest benefits of network marketing.

What's the difference between residual income and linear income?

Why is residual income better?

Linear income is income you earn when you work at a regular job. You are exchanging your time and skills for money–whatever amount of money the company is willing to pay for your time and skills. *They* decide what you're worth. *You don't.*

Residual income is money that you earn for long periods of time based on a one-time effort. That is *exactly* what happens in network marketing!

You may be familiar with the effects and benefits of residual income even if you've never heard the term. Let me give you some examples.

Think of Bill Gates in the world of computers, or Michael Jackson, Madonna, Laverne and Shirley and many other superstars in the music and show business, or Michael Jordan or Jerry Rice in the sports business. You hear about their "big contracts," but you don't hear about their residual income.

Let's take Michael Jackson. He's such big name that any time he records a CD, millions of copies are purchased. (The same is true for Madonna or any music-biz superstar.) You hear about how many million copies of the new Michael Jackson CD sold in the first weeks or months after the CD's release–and of course superstar Michael gets a cut from *every one* of his CDs sold. Ah, but it doesn't stop there! People are *still buying* every CD he's ever made that's still available. In 2001, or maybe 2010, people will still be buying a CD he made in 1998! For his one-time effort of recording that CD, he will earn money in the year 2001 and far

20

beyond–even if it's not a very good CD! People will buy it because Michael Jackson is a superstar whose name has been and will be well-marketed..

If Elvis Presley were still alive, he'd be earning residuals on every album he ever made. Today, those residuals go to his estate. His family benefits from his one-time effort to make those recordings.

Bill Gates is a slightly different case. People don't buy his Microsoft computer programs because they worship superstar Bill Gates. They buy Microsoft Windows because he's had the business and marketing savvy to make Windows the *de facto* standard for the way computers work. In the computer business, you can't stand still, so he isn't earning residual income from his first version of the DOS operating system (from which Windows grew). He's earning income on Microsoft's present product line because he made the ***one-time effort*** of convincing IBM to use DOS on their new PC–which became the *de facto* standard for all desktop and laptop computers! He was so successful that Apple, which many believe had and has better technology and better software (but as a company made classically terrible marketing decisions) now has less than ten percent of the market! Everything else runs on Bill Gates' (Microsoft's) Windows. He earns money every time a Microsoft product sells and every time a product which runs on Windows (90 percent of the market, remember) is sold!

Every time there's a rerun of *Laverne and Shirley* or *Happy Days* or any of those shows, Laverne and Shirley and the actors and actresses in those shows earns residual income. Every time those reruns go on TV, they get paid.

The problem, of course, is that most of us will never have the opportunity to be a superstar in the music or entertainment business, or in computers, athletics or such. But in network marketing you have the same residual income potential! You are *not* exchanging time for money!

All of the Forbes top 100 income earners earn residual income. ***They do not exchange time for money.***

21

Table 2.1: Traditional Product/Service Movement Versus Network Marketing

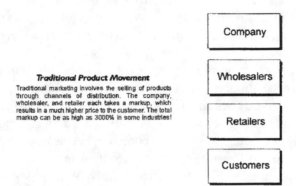

Traditional Product Movement

Traditional marketing involves the selling of products through channels of distribution. The company, wholesaler, and retailer each takes a markup, which results in a much higher price to the customer. The total markup can be as high as 3000% in some industries!

Network Marketing

Network marketing involves the selling of products through a network of independent distributors. Markup is typically 30% to 50%. This short channel of distribution keeps prices lower and quality higher. Customers receive much higher value.

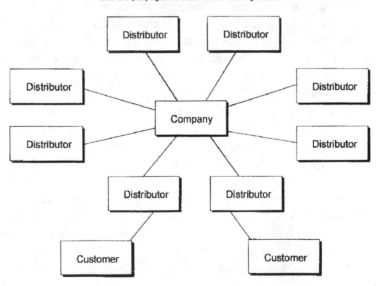

Ninety-five percent of all bankruptcies in this country could have been avoided if the person who went bankrupt had made *only an extra $400 a month!* Home-based network marketing could have provided that–and then some!

Still another advantage to network marketing is that you are helping consumers. They are buying products and services directly, without the middle man markup, which saves them money.

This is the way products and services will be purchased in 21st century. You are helping your customers get more out of their dollar, usually for a higher quality product or service than they could find elsewhere, at cost-effective prices per use, and with a more convenient delivery system! (Can anyone beat that?)

Let me give you the example of a box of breakfast cereal. It costs ten *cents* or so to make, but when you buy it at the supermarket it costs two to four *dollars*. marketing and distribution costs, and the expense of keeping the grocery store open and staffed. You pay for that marketing and distribution. You pay the salaries of the managers and employees of that grocery store, and you pay for the shelf space, maintenance, liability insurance, theft, breakage, spoilage, etc., and especially the advertising budget. Millions upon millions of dollars *in advertising alone* are spent–*on just one product!*

During the SuperBowl, a thirty-second commercial costs a million dollars or more! (It goes up every year.) It's worth that price, and then some, to advertise Budweiser, Pepsi, cars, athletic shoes, and the other mass-market products you see during the SuperBowl. You may remember that Apple introduced the Macintosh computer with a SuperBowl commercial, in perhaps one of the most classic commercials of all time.

Nike athletic shoes cost from $3 to $5 to make in Taiwan, Indonesia, etc., but the average cost of a good pair of Nike or other quality athletic shoes in this country is $85! This is what it takes to pay for middle-man markups and store costs.

Yet another advantage of network marketing is you don't need an office.

You can work from home. You don't have the cost of an office in some building. Better yet, the cost of your home office is tax-deductible! There is no need for babysitters to raise your kids. (Of course, if you're raising very young children, you may find that a lot of your productive time is diverted by their needs. It's not unheard of for a home-office worker to hire a babysitter to keep the kids out of the home office! But you can usually write that off, too!)

There's no commuting, which saves time and tolls, gas and fares. There's no expense and time relating to personal appearance and the clothing and time needed to look your very best for the office. (Both men and women can save a lot here.) As a home-based networker, the only time you need to look sharp and professional is when you're making a presentation or meeting someone from your company. You save on transportation, save the time you spend commuting, save costs of child care, food, etc. Your home office will save you money rather than be an overhead you have to carry, as you would in any other business. It becomes a tax write-off!

You are paid for the actions you perform for free every day of your life.

Let me talk about that for a moment.

You are already doing network marketing every single day of your life!

When you say to somebody, "Hey, did you see that new hit movie? That was a great film!" The person says, "No," and asks you to tell them about it (tell them why it's worth seeing), you've marketed that movie—*for free*! The studio counts on you to do that! Your comments get them interested, so they take their friends to see the film. You've made money for that movie theater and that movie. The people you talk to tell their friends, who go see the film, and they tell their friends, and so on—which is what happens in network marketing, *but in network marketing, you get paid!*

You're doing free marketing for an auto maker when you say to a friend with a new car, "Hey, that's a great car! I love it! Where did you buy it?" You're *asking* that person to market the car to you! Even if you don't buy the car, you may talk about it to friends. Your questions to others about products they use influences what you buy. Your comments about what you own and use influence other people to buy that automobile or that great dress, or that brand of coffee or whatever. (Walt, my editor, tells me that he's personally sold somewhere between fifty and a hundred copies of WordPerfect, his preferred word processing program. "But does WordPerfect pay me anything? *Not dime one!*") When you recommend a product or service you like, you're doing word-of-mouth advertising, suggesting that your friend should purchase this item or that, based on your own personal experiences and observations.

That's why when a movie is about to come out, it's heavily advertised–until it hits the theaters. After that, word-of-mouth is sufficient to bring movie-goers into the theater. You no longer see commercials for a movie after it hits the theaters, because there is no need to spend advertising dollars. (Of course it also works the other way–a heavily-advertised smash flop can't be salvaged by the best conventional ad campaign.)

Another advantage of network marketing is that *skills can be learned while you are making money*. Training is free. No four-year degrees. No tens of thousands of dollars spent on education. You can be making a profit in your first month. The average business break-even point is thirty-six months after startup–assuming it breaks even at all. Nine out of ten start-up businesses fail in their first five years.

In network marketing, you can make a profit in your first month.

Another advantage of network marketing is that you gain positive recognition for your accomplishments *immediately*.

Recognition is missing in corporate America. In home-based network marketing, instant recognition raises your ego and confidence. That helps you to be a better, happier, person, with a healthy attitude that rubs off on every area of your life and on everyone around you. It will improve your social skills. It will improve your communication skills. It will help your family life.

It will help your corporate career–as long as you continue to pursue it.

Your attitude determines *everything* in life, certainly including your health and wealth. It's very true that "If you believe you can, you will; if you believe you can't–you're right!"

All successful people, those who succeed in *anything* in life, from being a great parent to becoming the President of the United States, succeed because they have a positive attitude. Network marketing can improve your attitude until it's constantly positive, through recognition, receiving training, adopting common goals, making new friends, attending conventions, and hearing nationally-known motivational public speakers.

Networking, the key element of network marketing, allows you the freedom to choose who you want to work with. This is called *work with the willing*. You can choose to work with those who work like you and, *even more important*, you can choose to work with those you get along with! (I'm sure everyone has had the highly negative experience, some time in their lives, of working with someone who was difficult to get along with!) That makes this business fun to be part of and enjoyable in ways you may never have had the opportunity to experience.

You pick your partners. *You* choose the people you will work with and those you will not. You have the delightful anticipation of gain, with no fear of loss. *It is never boring!* Every day is different. Training and the experience of marketing to many kinds of people–to lawyers one day and homemakers the next–make home-based network marketing one of the most rewarding ways to make money that's ever been created. It's not that old line that "variety is the spice of life." In networking, *life is variety!* (The spices of life then take care of themselves!)

Who are your customers? Who are the people to whom you market? Well, it's extremely simple and very basic: **anyone with a pulse is qualified to be a customer of any network marketing company!**

That makes the target market unlimited! There are no routine over-and-over-and-over-again presentations.

You'll learn about all types of professions. In my years of network marketing I've learned about offshore trusts and corporate law from attorneys; nutrition from medical professionals; about the entertainment business from actors and musicians; and how to better raise your family from experts in that field. I relish all the benefits of gaining knowledge by meeting and talking to a broad spectrum of people I'd never meet in any other business.

You're in a business where most of the financial backing and legal resources–accounting, bookkeeping, manufacturing, distribution, accounts payable, accounts receivable, firing, hiring, licensing, patent costs, overhead, order takers, satellite broadcasts, marketing experts, packaging, shelf space and risk–are assumed by the company, its CEO, and its corporate staff.

Network marketing is the only business I know that offers unlimited residual income potential without the downside risks of owning a typical business.

In network marketing there is no limit to your income. If you have written down your goals, have an action plan for your daily activities and follow it (for example how many presentations you need to make each day and when you will make them), your income potential is unlimited!

You are not exchanging time for money as you would in a typical job or business you might own. That's linear income. You start each day where you left off yesterday. The great benefit of working for commissions is that the more you market the products and services to more potential customers and members of your network, the more money you make. Your attitude must be focused on how you build your business. Your attitude will determine the degree and speed of your success.

If you believe you will make $5,000 a month–or $20,000 a month–in network marketing, that's half the battle. As the saying goes, some people think the glass is half full and some think it is half empty. Those who think the glass is half full have a much better chance of maximizing their income in this business–or in any business.

Imagine that you train ten people in your organization. They each commit ten hours a week to working at their business, and they meet their commitment.

You are earning money on one hundred hours of marketing each week.

If you continue to enroll new customers and build your downline, those numbers could be 100 x 10 or even 1,000 x 10 each week. This makes network marketing a business of unlimited potential.

I'll summarize what I've said in this chapter with some points listing the major advantages of becoming part of the of network marketing industry.

- The startup cost is low. To get involved, your greatest need is your willingness to commit yourself and your time.

- You escape the headaches of typical businesses.

- There are great tax advantages.

- You have both time freedom and financial freedom.

- The powers of duplication and leverage are constantly working for you.

- Anyone can become successful.

- You are your own boss.

- You have unlimited income potential.

- Residual income is created...and lasts...and lasts.

- You are helping customers get a better product and/or service at a lower price, more conveniently.

- You have positive income flow immediately and form great friendships as partnerships are established.

What is Network Marketing?

Network Marketing is the movement of products or services directly from the manufacturer to the end user, who hears about the products or services via *word of mouth*. You've been involved in networking all your life without knowing it. Every time you tell your friends about a good movie, a nice restaurant, or a sale going on in the mall, you're networking. *You're marketing that business or product* via *word of mouth*.

As I said earlier, you may have noticed that movies are usually heavily advertised *before* they open in theaters. Once a film hits the theaters, relatively little money is spent on advertising, especially TV advertising. Full-page newspaper ads, often paid for by the film production companies, are replaced by smaller ads bought by theaters showing the film or no ads at all. The movie will be promoted predominantly by word-of-mouth advertising. That kind of marketing is free to the movie companies–and they consider it the best kind of marketing they can get. We do networking all the time for almost every product or service we use–*and we do it for free!*

In network marketing, *you are paid* for doing this form of advertising on a *residual income* basis.

What is Residual Income?

Residual income is income you continue to earn for a long period of time as a result of marketing a product or service once.

You continue to make money from that product or service every time someone in your organization, whom you may or may not know, sells (markets) it to a customer–whom you also don't know. You receive money for work you did weeks, months, or years earlier, when you convinced someone else to become part of your

29

network. That person convinced someone else to become part of their network (and therefore part of your network), and the new person sold the product or service to the customer–who may also become part of that person's network, and part of your network. The person may become a customer–they buy and use the product or service–or they may become a business builder and go out to add more people to their network and yours. I'll talk about the difference between customers and business builders, and the importance of each, later.

You continue to be rewarded for the work you did in the past to bring others into the business.

When you purchase an insurance policy, the person who sold you the policy is paid a residual commission every time you renew your insurance. *As long as you keep your insurance with that company and agent, the agent gets paid.*

In other kinds of commissioned selling, such as the work of real estate agents or car salespeople, the person doing the marketing and making the sale **gets paid only once.** *There is no residual income from selling a house or car.*

In network marketing an *average everyday person* like you can create a residual income stream by word-of-mouth advertising of a company's products or services. Networking can work for *anyone and everyone.*

Residual income recipients like insurance agents require unique or special talent or education–or both–to earn their money. In networking, you don't need a college degree or any special talent but the ability to talk to people to earn residual income.

Residual income is the only way I've ever seen which ensures that you will have the money to enjoy your free time, and that you will have free time, once you have an organization and a strong customer base. Most people you and I know enjoy *either* free time *or* plenty of money–or neither–**but not both.**

I've taught hundreds of people how to accomplish what most people only dream of–to not only have no money worries, but also to have the time to enjoy it with your family and friends.

That's how powerful network marketing is!

What's an Illegal Pyramid Scheme?

"Is your company one of those illegal pyramids?"

That's a question I hear all the time, perhaps the most frequently asked question in networking.

No, networking isn't illegal. Nor are all pyramid-structured businesses illegal. Let me explain.

Every company, the U.S. government, and virtually any organization of any kind, uses a pyramid organizational structure.

In a company there is usually one president, several senior vice presidents, then VPs of different departments or areas of the world, senior managers, managers, and assistant managers. How many layers exist in this pyramid structure depends in part on how big the company is, but employees are *always* at the bottom of the company pyramid.

The same goes for the government, where the President holds the highest position and the heads of each governmental agency report directly to him or through a member of his cabinet.

Even a social organization, whether it's the Rotary Club, the Business and Professional Women, the PTA, or the Symphony Board, has a pyramid organizational structure.

You can see that the pyramid structure not only works, but it's also normally perfectly legal and is accepted without a second thought.

A pyramid-structured business *can* be illegal *under certain conditions* when the structure is used for purposes that are *illegal under the law*. That's what's meant when someone talks about illegal pyramid schemes–and they are indeed schemes, created with the intent that those on top will make all the money and all others who participate never figure it out. That's the kind of organization that has given the term "pyramid" a bad name.

Federal law defines an illegal pyramid as a business venture where a person must *make an investment* to get the *right to recruit others into a company*. Such a person receives money *solely* from recruiting people. The new recruits *must make an investment*.

There is *no* ongoing or residual income The new recruits *make money from others* when they recruit others to join. All these conditions must be in place for the law to consider a business an *illegal* pyramid.

A simple definition of an illegal pyramid is a business where money is made from signing up new people rather than by marketing and selling legitimate products or services to end-user consumers.

An example of an illegal pyramid is when someone asks you to invest $1,000. In exchange, the person tells you that if you recruit two people to each invest $1,000, and each of those two people gets two people to invest $1,000, and each of those four people now gets two people each to invest $1,000, you will then be paid $14,000 when you reach the top of the money tree. Why? Fourteen people are in your money downline, each paying $1,000 for their spot in the pyramid, in the hope that they will also get to the top of the money pyramid.

This is an *illegal* pyramid because:

1. Those at the bottom of the pyramid will get burned
2. No legitimate product or service is being sold.
3. You are being paid *only* for recruiting others.
That's illegal.

It's also a very dirty business practice. Could you sleep at night if you did that to someone who trusted you enough to put up $1,000? I couldn't.

What is Your Upline?

Your *upline* in the company you join consists of the people directly above you in the organization. (You are part of the upline of people in your downline.)

Let's say you were signed up by Bob.

Bob is a member of your upline.

However, Bob was signed up by Mary, and Mary was signed up by Tim. So, Mary and Tim are also members of your upline. Some members of your upline will be compensated for your monthly purchases. When you recruit other customers, depending on your status with the company and how closely they are connected to you in the company's compensation plan, you will be compensated based on what they purchase. They, in turn, will be compensated based on the purchases of customers they recruit, and the purchases of customers those customers recruit, and so on. Everyone in the organization is compensated based on the sale (and purchase) of products, *not solely on the basis of how many people they recruit.*

Learn who your upline is (above the person who signed you up), as soon as possible. Try to schedule an appointment with them so you can be trained in the company's system, methods, and products. Try to get them to help you with your first few presentations. Remember, you make money for your upline, so make them work for it. Expect to do the same for members of your downline as your organization grows. Try to find an active member on your upline who shares your excitement about building a customer base. Team up with that person.

What Is Your Downline?

Your *downline* consists of the people who are under you in the organization. They are the exact opposite of an upline–and you have the same responsibility to them that you expect your upline to have to you.

Anyone you sign up personally is in your downline. When you help that person sign up new customers of his or her own, and those people sign up others, all those people are in your downline. Thus if you sign up Jennifer, and she signs up Louis, and Louis signs up Evan, all three are part of your downline. Everyone they sign up is also part of your downline.

If you're good at duplicating your efforts and work hard with the right people, your downline can become exponentially large. This means that six tiers down from you there could be hundreds–or even *thousands*–of people marketing the company's products or services, using the word-of-mouth approach.

CHAPTER THREE

YOUR FIRST TEST: CHOOSE YOUR PARTNER AND DANCE

There are thousands of network marketing companies to choose from. At first glance, many of them look like good opportunities. If you *have already chosen a company*, this chapter will help you make certain you're with the right opportunity. If you *have not* chosen a company, this chapter will help you make the right choice. Before we get into how to select the right company, let's go through some background facts.

Ninety percent of all networking companies fail inside eighteen months. Only *one* out of 1,000 is left in five years! Just like all typical businesses, most networking companies will not make it. You obviously don't want be involved with a network marketing failure! Your time, money, reputation and financial goals and dreams are at stake.

When I first learned of this industry, I developed a *personal wish list* for what I wanted from the company I would join. Later, I realized my list defined the success factors that need to be in place to have a good network marketing opportunity. My wish list had every point I believed at that time, and learned and confirmed later, that a network marketing company needs to have in place to assure that it will last for my lifetime and the lifetimes of the members of my organization.

At the time, I didn't know whether such a company existed–but I was not going to get involved unless I found one. After extensive research on over one hundred of the best opportunities in this industry, and spending thousands of dollars on travel, running Dun

& Bradstreet reports, going to many State Attorney General's offices, and meeting the CEOs and corporate management teams of many companies, I chose the company I'm now with. I believed it was the company that could make my wishes come true. It has certainly done that!

The first success factor to look for is a company with a track record.

Usually, you should look for a networking company that's over five years old. If you get into a business that started last month, last year, or even three years ago, it becomes very risky. It's not quite like playing the lottery, but close. As I said above, approximately one network marketing company in a thousand makes it to five years. You might get lucky, and certainly there are benefits to being in on the ground floor, but the odds of getting into the *right* company in its infancy are not good at all. If you want to gamble, that's your choice, but *know the risks!*

Other disadvantages of most ground-floor opportunities are that there are no good training materials for you to duplicate and distribute. There are no tapes, workbooks, seminars, or conventions you and your organization can attend. This is a common problem for any company in its infancy. Another very serious problem is that products and services may not be delivered in a timely manner–an instant turn-off to most people you might bring into your organization. Pricing is rarely competitive. The company needs high production (which can't happen until it generates a high volume of business) to lower the per-unit cost of each item it markets.

The company has no proven track record. That lowers its credibility to those you contact and makes it harder for you to recruit new members for your organization.

When you can show prospective members a bunch of average people who are earning great part-time and full-time income in your opportunity, that's a powerful incentive for a new person to join your organization. This helps to excite and motivate prospective new members to join. It convinces them that the payoff is there if they put in the same level of hard work that brought success to you and others in your organization.

A young company may have cash flow problems. Your checks, *and those for the members of your organization*, may not come on time. Obviously, that will cause major dissatisfaction within your downline organization and be a frequent reason for dropouts.

The company's products and services have not yet been used on a large scale. What if they haven't been adequately tested and some people are allergic to them? What if the manufacturer doesn't produce the product fast enough? These are common problems of new companies. The company needs to work through those problems. That does not and cannot happen instantly or overnight. It may take the first few years, or longer. That's something you do not want any part of.

For that matter, check out the stability and track record of companies which have been around a while–you want to be sure they've solved all those problems, and have not developed new problems.

As Walt, the old journalist, says, "The first thing I learned on the first day of News Reporting 101, way back in 1957, was: *'Never assume! Check it out.'* That was good advice then. It's good advice now."

That's why my wish and my recommendation is that you go with a company that's been in business for at least five years.

My second wish was to find a financially strong business. If the company is privately held, you can run a Dun & Bradstreet report which shows you how strong the company is. Look for a 4A1 or a 5A1 rating. The 4 and 5 stand for the size of the company. The A1 shows that the company has no long-term debt. If the business has no long-term debt, it is a good sign the business will last. You can get a D&B at some office supply stores, or at financial institutions like a bank or S&L.

If the company you are researching is publicly held, ask for an annual report. You can and should go to the Better Business Bureau and the Attorney General in your area to do a background check on the company. You want to learn how many complaints and/or lawsuits have been filed against the company.

Look for a company that's squeaky clean!

That means it has no long-term debt, the company has prepaid for expansion of plant and manufacturing space and there have not been many complaints in the past or present. If a company had complaints in the past, but the last few years are clean, it *may* be a sign that the executive managers have solved their problems and cleaned up their act–but check them out further before joining. *Never assume, remember?*

The third success factor for a company is a good management team. The CEO is the first person to check out. Talk to him or her if you can. Look at his/her past marketing, corporate, and educational experience. He or she is the captain of the ship. You want someone who can help you get to a great financial destination smoothly and quickly.

Learn the answers to these questions when you meet him or her:

1. Is he or she honest, integrity-based and fair?

2. Does he or she have a commitment to and vision of building a business to last a lifetime?

3. How much of the company does he or she own?

4. Does he or she have a long-term vision?

5. Is he or she a delegating or an on-the-job leader?

6. Can you talk to the CEO at all? If not, be cautious.

Look at the corporate management team. This is the supporting cast that helps guide the captain. In the nautical terms I've been using, these people are the first and second mate, the bosun, the chief engineer, etc. These are the people who make it happen for the captain–and for you. Check the VPs' and managers' backgrounds. Look for how much marketing experience in the direct sales industry they had before they joined this organization. Will they be hands-on with you and your distributor force?

You need to do all this checking because you are making one of the biggest business decisions of your life. You will be investing time, money, contacts, your reputation, and your personal effort in this business. If you believe it was smart to spend quality time looking for your mate, your first home, a new car, or a new job, the same focus needs to be placed on this decision. Your job is to sift through a lot of dirt to find your gold nugget.

That gold nugget is the company that will provide you with a residual income forever.

Because I did that kind of research, I joined a business that *has helped thousands* of average working individuals make extra monthly part-time income.

As I said in Chapter Two, ninety percent of all personal bankruptcies would never happen if that person had an extra $400 a month. The difference between good living and disaster *really can* be that small!

If you pick the right company, you can be responsible for training hundreds or maybe even thousands of people who some day will begin making extra income forever. You can be one of them.

The fourth success factor to look for in a network marketing company offers a unique, consumable, product or service–at reasonable prices.

If you market non-consumables, you're in sales, just like a realtor or car salesman–or the overworked, underpaid clerk in a department store. *That* type of marketing means that at the beginning of each month you start at zero sales and zero residuals. (And the department store clerk may not even earn a commission at all, depending on store policy.)

Many marketing companies preach no selling, retailing, distributing or inventory. However, with a non-consumable product or service, that is *exactly* what you have to do! You may not have inventory–say cases of soap stacked to the rafters of your garage–but if you want your income to continue, much less to grow, you must make new sales each day and each month. You are in the distributing and retailing business! Every day, you have to go out and do it again. *There is no residual income.*

You REALLY want to market a consumable!

I can't stress that too much!

Marketing consumables allows you to establish a customer for a specific product (or products) line or service, because of your one-time presentation. That person, *even if they are a zero on the scale I used in Chapter One, a person who brings no one else into your organization,* will make you money over and over and over again, every time he or she orders more of the products and/or services! (Is that powerful, or what?)

The difference between marketing consumable and non-consumable items is that consumables create residual (ongoing) income from re-orders, but non-consumables are purchased once, and therefore are sold only once. Non-consumables produce no residual income or repeat business.

Suppose you market diligently and develop one hundred new customers this month. What happens next month? If you market non-consumables and plan to make the same amount of money you made in the previous month, you have to sell the item to one hundred new customers. And do it again the next month, and so on, month after month, if you want your income to continue.

If you market a consumable product or service to those same one hundred new customers, a percentage of these customers will call an 800 number and re-order. You won't get all one hundred to place a new order the next month–some will not see a benefit in the product or service, some will not use all of the supply they bought, and some will be lazy and forget. You'll get a percentage of ongoing repeat business from those one hundred customers, and a percentage from the one hundred (or whatever number) you develop next month and the month after, and so on.

You can see that this can rapidly add up to a lot of residual income. *Repeat orders for the same product or service is what makes your income residual.*

How much residual income you generate depends on the uniqueness and the quality of what you are marketing. If what you offer cannot be easily purchased anywhere else, the loyalty rate of your customer base increases. If the quality of your product is better than the competition, this also goes a long way to developing a loyal customer base. The bigger that base, the more residual income you make.

And you add to your residual income base each month!

The growth principle is the same as the "penny doubled each day" example I used earlier.

How do You Choose a Good Company?

Check it out! Check out the products! Try the products and/or services yourself. Look at the cost, the competition, the quality and convenience. Ask yourself every question you can imagine a potential customer would ask–the same questions you'd ask if you were the customer.

Is the packaging attractive and professional? Are the products better than those you're using now? Do they really save you and everybody else money per use or per container? How long did it take to deliver these products to your home? How much was the shipping charge? A shipping and handling charge of more than ten percent of the cost of the order is too high. Are the products environmentally safe? Are they hypoallergenic? Are they staple products and services which appeal to all or most people, or do they appeal only to a limited number of people? How many items are there to choose from? It is very advantageous for you if the company offers thirty or more products. By offering that many products the company increases your chances that potential customers will find one or more products or services to their liking (and increases its own long-term stable profit potential, which is important to you).

There should be at least two *sizzle products*. Sizzle products are those which have instant appeal and are unique. Their patents or trademarks make them exclusive. The customer can't get them anywhere else. These products should have clear and demonstrable benefits for all who use them, and those benefits should be evident within several weeks of use.

Sizzle products are what initially give customers a motivating reason to join your network marketing company. However, a successful marketing operation always has a good variety of everyday items that everyone needs and uses.

The company creates a great marketing situation when it enables customers to spend *no new money*. Your customers simply **redirect their spending** *to the products of the company you represent*, buying the same kinds of products from that company that they used to purchase at grocery and drug stores–or wherever similar products or services are sold or marketed. You and your customers are purchasing higher-quality products without spending new money, and perhaps are even saving money.

Health care products, for one example, are highly consumable. That makes them great products to offer. People are becoming more health conscious every day. As baby boomers age, they care more about what they eat and how they are taking care of themselves physically. This influences younger consumers as well–the children of baby boomers are learning from their parents!

Health care products are a booming industry.

Vitamins, just one part of the health care product industry, are highly desirable to have in your line. Vitamins are a fifty *billion-dollar-a-year* industry! You don't need a marketing consultant to tell you there's a *huge* market! Vitamins are as consumable as you can get. If you don't take them, they don't do you any good! When the bottle is empty, you have to buy more to continue to get their benefit. That makes them great products to market.

Personal care products are also great to market. Yes, lotions and potions. They are consumable necessities which everyone needs. Even in the Great Depression of the 1930's, the personal care products industry was one of the few that *did not lose sales!*

Imagine making money each time someone takes a shower, brushes their teeth and uses soap, shampoo, conditioner, and deodorant!

Home hygiene offers another great group of products. These cleaning products should be hypoallergenic, all natural, and have a low cost per use.

I recommend that you stay away from faddish products like dietary supplements or non-proven cancer or heart products from which people might or might not see benefits.

As I said above, the company you choose should have a sizzle product or two. You need a unique product to convince those who hesitate that you offer something they can't get anywhere else. Unique, patented products do a good job of drawing people into your chosen networking company.

Learn whether there is good literature to accompany these products. Does the literature explain the product and market its unique benefits? Does the company manufacture its products, or does it depend on an outside supplier?

The best network marketing scenario is one in which the company *offers both products and services.* Very few companies that market only services but offer no products make it, long-term. Service-only companies are risky ventures. It's good to offer services in addition to products because of the purchasing power and customer base you have with networking businesses. Imagine what can happen to your income if the network marketing company you are looking at has 100,000 customers and offers both products and services to your customers! Most likely, the service will save you and your customers money, because of the sheer purchasing power a company with a large customer base offers the service provider.

For example, AAA can offer great prices on roadside assistance because it offers the tow-truck companies so much business. The tow truck companies can charge AAA less per service call because they make it up from savings resulting from the high volume of service AAA buys from them. A tow truck that's always on the road is a lot more efficient and profitable than one which makes a service call, returns to base, waits for another call, and goes out whenever a call comes–if one does.

The same principle applies when a network marketing company offers a service. The service provider can charge the marketing company less because it will not incur the costs of marketing to the network company's established customer base. Therefore, the network marketing company can offer a great deal to you and your customers. If you can offer your present and potential customers a service or two that they already use–perhaps can't live without–at a better price than they're getting now, you've given that customer a powerful reason to remain in your organization and continue to buy the products and services you offer. Best of all, the service is one more source of residual income!

The more products and services you have to market, the better. If you have many streams of income, you will have something to offer anybody and everybody; you will have ways to make something you're marketing appeal to almost everyone you meet.

Can the company expand its products and services markets internationally? A company with that potential, or one which has just begun international marketing, is a company that's going somewhere and will offer you the opportunity to go with it.

Is the networking company focused on its products and services, or is it focused on signing up people? *That is, is it product-centered or recruitment-centered?* **You want a company that is product-centered!**

A company that's signing-up centered is a house of cards. It's a scam waiting to collapse. It may well be an illegal pyramid. A product-centered company is long-term-dedicated to building its business and yours, and the businesses of the people you sign up, to last a lifetime.

Will all the products be available, to assure that supply keeps up with the demand?

What percentage of the company's profit goes into research and development (R&D)? You want a company that puts a substantial amount of its profits back into the research and development of new products and continued testing and improvement of existing products. Are new products and services announced every three to six months? Does the company have good scientists and product developers, along with great marketers, to effectively introduce new products into the distributor force?

It's been said that good marketing can sell anything. There's a large measure of truth in that–but *only* in the short term! Regardless of how well a product is marketed, if it doesn't live up to its promises, failure is guaranteed. The greatest marketing in the world can't prevent long-term failure. The company's scientists and research staff are just as important to your success as its marketing plan! You must have good products if you expect long-term success. You want a *product-centered company*!

A *major* success factor you should look for *and demand* from a company is a reasonable personal production requirement.

This is important not only to your success but to the success of those you bring into your organization. If you, and the people in your organization, have to meet an unreasonable production target, you'll find yourself with a high drop-out rate–and may well give up yourself. Some companies require you to *personally* purchase $1,000 or more of products a month in order to qualify to earn money from the efforts of the people in your organization. *I feel this is incredibly un-duplicatable*. It's also very unfair.

The average family in the United States earns $42,000 a year. That sharply limits how much most people can invest each month in products and sales tools.

The reasons most people decide to join your organization (or any networking company) are low start-up cost and great residual income potential.

High attrition–a lot of people quitting and dropping out of your organization–will occur when the start-up and ongoing costs are high. Also, high costs mean a low sign-up rate–which isn't what you're looking for in a company!

Ask yourself whether you would feel good if you enrolled your mother, your best friend and your neighbor in this business. If there are huge quotas with high attrition, most people will fail. You would not want to enroll your family, friends, or anyone else in that type of business.

You want a monthly sales quota that can be used by an average-sized family each month. A zero-quota is bad, because this promotes no product-centeredness, no loyalty to the backbone of the company–and no incentive to sell.

A reasonably low quota is desirable and necessary for the following reasons:

1. It redirects spending and allows people to become product centered. They buy the same products from the company that they'd buy from conventional sources–the supermarket or drugstore, for example–but spend their money with the company instead. Often, they get lower prices and/or better quality, which provide incentives to stay with the company. A low quota means there is no inventory loading–you don't have stacks of unsold products stored in your garage that you don't use and can't sell.

2. No new money is needed to participate in the company's compensation plan. You make money without needing to spend a lot of up-front money to qualify to be compensated. (Check the details of each plan.) People you sign up just redirect expenses that you and the members of your organization already have to better and/or lower cost products.

3.   It makes marketing executives product centered. They use and love the products and services they're teaching you market. If you are marketed to by a marketing executive who is personally using the products and services, you have more confidence in that person, the company, and your ability to use and market the products and services. Everyone who is marketing the products and services is personally using them.

4.   This is duplicatable. Most people can use products but not sell products. Ninety-seven percent of everybody in this country hates to sell–and they hate to ask someone to pay a bill even more. A no-collection system–that is, the company bills and collects the payments–is based on people *ordering and using* products, whether they choose to become business builders or are happy to just be customers.

5.   You can build a business to last a lifetime, *based on the products*. The products are the backbone of the company, *not the compensation plan*. The compensation plan grows from the products, not the other way around.

6.   There is a high sign-up ratio, which means you will be able to build your business more easily and rapidly than with a plan that generates low sign-ups–like most plans which require a large up-front investment. There are fewer obstacles, because almost everybody can accept simply redirecting expenses, that is, using a different source for products and services they already need, use, and want. Few people will sign up if they have to sell directly and collect payments.

7.   You can feel good that your customers will not be financially hurt. You can introduce the products and services, and the company's system, to everyone who has hair or skin–and not necessarily even both. You know that the products and services have universal appeal, and meet the needs and pocketbooks of almost everyone. You know that all the other marketers in the company *really are*

using what they are preaching. Imagine if you went to a Toyota dealership and learned that the Toyota salesperson drives a Honda to work. You would probably think less of that Toyota salesman and the whole operation. If a person who actually drives a Toyota is selling Toyotas, you would feel better about that person. You want everyone in your organization, both above and below you, to use the products they are marketing. As a home-based marketer, you should *"be a product of the product"* you are marketing!

8. It promotes a large number of people doing a little bit. John Paul Getty said it best when he said he would rather have one percent of a hundred people's efforts than one hundred percent of himself.

9. There is *a higher reorder rate* with a low personal production requirement. You and your people–customers and business builders alike–can order what they need. They do not feel constant pressure to sell. High-pressure sales are neither necessary nor encouraged. How many people enjoy encountering high-pressure sales tactics, much less enjoy using those tactics themselves?

This brings me to another major factor by which to measure a company's success; one that's high on my wish list. Look for a company with a high reorder rate. You should think of a high reorder rate as a high loyalty rate.

Reorder rates measure the percentage of existing customers who continue to order *every* month, *after* the month in which they joined. Most networking companies have a reorder rate of between ten and thirty percent. This means that during any given month, out of every hundred customers you have in your business, ten to thirty customers will reorder. The rest will not. The higher the reorder rate the better. To find out the reorder rate, ask top marketers in the company you are researching, the people who are possibly your future upline, to show you or tell you about their monthly reorder rate.

The advantages of a high reorder rate are:

1. High residuality. If people continue to purchase the products each month and there is a high reorder rate for them, you earn a high residual income simply because you are earning money on past efforts.

2. You have a one-time build. That means you are building a business to last a lifetime based on the ongoing *reorders* of customers rather than on the ongoing *replacement* of customers. A constant need to replace customers does not allow you to retire–and is very frustrating.

3. There is less frustration from your leaders. Replacing inactive customers is very de-motivating. This is a big reason why networkers give up.

4. A high reorder rate shows that what you are marketing is cost-effective, high in quality, and conveniently and promptly delivered. That's a powerful sign that the company has an excellent chance to last for many years.

5. A high reorder rate allows the company to plan more effectively and economically. Its personnel, procurement, manufacturing, production, shipping, materials, and ingredients can be managed to make the company more efficient. This keeps down the cost of the products.

6. A high reorder rate also allows the company to spend more money on research and development and expand its product line. The managers know profits are consistent, so they can commit the research money to expand their line and keep the company growing and responsive to customers' needs. This allows the company to grow at a healthy and profitable pace. This success factor is one of the most important to analyze. Don't join a network

marketing company until you see that the business reports of many top leaders show their reorder rate is high.

The seventh success factor, a low initial investment, *must be present* before you join any networking company. I've talked about it earlier, and must stress its importance. Networking companies have initial investments ranging from $0 to $10,000 or more. The initial investment should include product and sales aid material, but beware—some companies with high fees will try to convince you that the high cost is to cover their expenses for their (claimed) "excellent" marketing and sales-aid materials. If *they* have to charge *you* for the cost of *their* marketing, you should wonder about the quality of their products, and the quality of the support you can expect them to provide you.

A company with zero investment sounds attractive at first, but there are a lot of reasons I recommend staying away from those companies.

Reason 1: The people in your downline are less committed. There is less commitment in your upline, and less within these companies themselves. The reorder rate will almost certainly be low. You should imagine, no matter what company you join, that you have just invested one million of your own hard-earned dollars to become a member. This will keep you focused and dedicated to that networking business.

Reason 2: There is a small profit center for the company. The company will stay in business only as long as its profit centers produce. If one profit center dries up, or a competitor does it better, the company dries up, too.

Reason 3: You have little or no business or training material going out to new customers. You have no materials and no support for your efforts to train and develop the potential business builders who will help build your organization. The progress of their success will be slowed or stopped by the lack of this material. A networking company with a high start-up cost, say $500 or more, has different problems–but the problems are equally hard to deal with.

Problem 1: People can and will get financially hurt if they cannot sell or use their initial product purchases. This places great strain on family relationships, and results in lost friendships. These bad-business issues cause severe hardships for you and everyone in your organization.

Problem 2: This high investment is not easily duplicatable. Some of your contacts cannot afford this initial investment. That prevents some good potential business builders from joining.

Problem 3: When marketers find themselves stuck with unsold and un-sellable inventory, some will contact the Better Business Bureau and the State Attorney General's office. A class-action law suit may be filed. This will give a company a bad reputation. As you know, bad news spreads faster than good news.

Problem 4: With companies like this, money is made from signing people up. The profit–for the company, not for you–is in the large initial investment made when people sign up, and the large inventories they are required to purchase. This form of compensation is not consistent, long-term, or residual. On the contrary, these companies call it "promotional volume." That's good only in the short run.

As I said earlier, you want to find a networking company which requires a start-up cost between $50 and no more than $1,000. This guarantees several benefits:

First, you and the people you sign up (business builders and customers alike) get something substantial upon joining your organization. They become product centered and learn more about the business before entering into it.

Second, those who join can't get hurt financially, since they are simply purchasing a consumable supply of products they'd use anyway, which they would otherwise buy from the company's competition. Neither you nor members of your organization can lose money. Nothing you or they are buying will be stacked to the ceiling of your garage or theirs six months from now. You and your people will buy only what *you and they* need and will consume. Neither you nor they will buy more than is needed.

Third, anyone can get involved. There is no price discrimination, that is, no high initial costs to join and no high monthly costs to continue. Anyone can participate without the risk of digging themselves into some deep financial hole if they do not continue marketing the items this company offers. People are not "committed" to giving this business a good effort because of the initial cost they incurred (fear of losing their money–fear is *always* a negative motivator), but because they understand the benefits of using the products, and the benefits the people they sign up will enjoy. The motivation to succeed is positive. As a result, all or most of your income will be residual and not based on promotional materials.

Before You Commit

Before you commit yourself to a business, ask these questions:

Will I be able to get my money back? Can anyone I introduce to this be hurt financially? Is my motive for signing up people to get a promotional bonus or to create a the foundation for obtaining long-term residual income for myself and my downline partners? Will people get their money's worth for joining? Will there be any inventory or unused items that I or my organization will be asked to purchase?

The perfect system, I believe, is to have a few initial investment options. A customer should be able to join as a member–like they might join BJ's, Price Club or Costco–at a cost of between $30 and $35, for which they will get reading materials, a product catalog, and an 800 number to call in orders. For part-time business builders, a sampler kit should be available with business materials and full-sized packages of some of the products. It should be available for between $100 and $300, and should cover the membership fee. For the more aggressive marketer, who has at least twenty hours a week to work at the business, an expanded $300 to $1,000 package of products and business materials is a real benefit, if it's available.

These graduated levels of entry offer affordable entry points intended to fit everyone's needs, depending on their interest level, time availability, and financial capability.

Check the Compensation Plan

The next major factor for your success, which you *must* look at, *closely*, is the compensation plan. Look at the details. *Take time to read the fine print!* Ask for explanations of anything you don't understand.

The compensation plan should have a number of key features. It should be set up to provide you with most of your profit coming from money earned as residual income. Look for low profit percentages on the promotional end or in one-time bonuses, since high figures on that kind of compensation usually mean you get less residual income. It could mean that the company's profits are based on sign-ups rather than actual sales. You want to make money on reorders from your customer base each month.

Remember, residual income is the best way to earn! It sure beats working at your old job!

I would rather make a percentage on a person's monthly purchases for the rest of his or her life than receive a one-time, up-front big bonus on a customer's initial order. Let me give you an example.

You want to look for a company that has an *equally-distributed marketing plan*. In such a plan there are cash carrots at the low, middle and upper levels of the compensation plan. "Equally distributed" does not mean everyone makes the same amount, but that the opportunity to earn is equally distributed at all levels.

Some companies have top income earners making $400,000 or more *a month* (!!!), but ninety-five percent or more of the people in their organization make little because the company is set up to funnel all the profits to the top.

Most networking companies pay out between forty and seventy percent on every dollar, since they have no advertising costs. Look for a top marketer who makes $50,000 to $100,000 a month. Ask that person, "How many hundreds of people in your organization are making an extra $1,000 a month? How many are making $3,000, $5,000, $10,000 or $20,000 a month?"

If the person says there are many people earing that kind of income, you know your organization will last forever because it's based on an equally distributed compensation plan.

Would you rather make $200,000 a month for two years and have it go up and down like a roller coaster, eventually fading away, or would you rather make a $50,000 a month income for a lifetime? I would rather have lifetime income, because you can count on it and know that, for the long run, it is a better situation to be in.

Look for a compensation plan that, in addition to residual income on the commissions, has perks for volume and sales increases. Look for a company that has a *revenue*-sharing (not a *profit*-sharing) program. This is where you participate in the company's growth.

Look for a business that has cash bonuses as immediate short-term incentives to keep people focused on increasing their sales volume.

Look for a business that has a car incentive. A company-bonus car is a concrete example of the success and lifestyle achieved by the middle and upper level people. This has a very strong motivating impact on your organization.

Look for a compensation plan with advancement perks, where there is always a carrot right in front of you to keep you moving and focused on increasing your sales volume–and which will keep members of your organization focused and moving. If you see a compensation plan that is *multi-dimensional* and *equally distributed*, you are looking at a good opportunity.

Once you find this company, there are many choices about the type of structure you can choose to plug into.

The most common are:

The Breakaway Marketing System

In a breakaway marketing system, everyone you enroll is on your first line, or directly under you. You are paid a residual on the group sales volume of these leaders.

Leaders are people who have reached leadership status because their sales volume reached a certain level.

Once a leader reaches a certain position in sales volume and productivity, either or both of two things can happen:

1. You can earn a lower percentage of the sales volume of that leader or,

2. If you have not reached a certain status level, that leader and his or her entire organization will be lost to you forever. That leader "breaks away" from your organization, hence the term, "breakaway marketing."

The reason breakaways work this way is that they truly allow you to create duplication, which is one of the keys to success in this industry. There is a huge benefit in this type of marketing system. It *forces* you to learn and assume *immediate leadership*, and *leadership is the force that will grow your business faster*.

Your leadership will create more independent leaders in your business.

Table 1.1: The Breakaway Plan

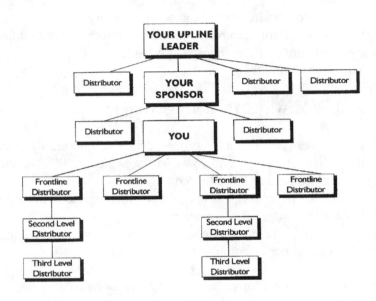

The other big benefit of a breakaway is that it allows powerful business builders, who may start out four levels apart, to end up working together directly, one under the other. That assures teamwork. This is what creates the big incomes made by the leaders in this structure. The concept behind the breakaway system is duplication.

The breakaway marketing system gives the advantage to leaders who break away. If they break away from *you*, you lose the residual income *they* produce.

If *you* are the breakaway leader you can make tremendous profits, but there are a few negatives in this system. In my opinion, the negatives include:

1. Part-time people who recruit an aggressive marketer may lose all the effort they put into that individual's business when that person breaks away.
2. Income is not usually equally distributed.
3. High attrition of customers is common in a breakaway system. Part-time leaders, who are critical to your organization, are not rewarded. Few people develop a walk-away flow of income that will last forever.

The Binary Marketing Plan

This newer type of marketing plan limits the number of first level distributors you can sponsor, but you are paid on your group sales volume to infinity. The average person in network marketing sponsors 2.3 people in the life of their membership in any program. (Have you ever wondered how you could enroll .3 of a person? Or what .3 of a child looks like in census statistics that claim most people have some figure like 2.3 children? Aren't statistics wonderful?) Binaries vary, but most plans allow you to put two or three on your first level. If you are an active business builder and enroll more than 2.3 (or 3) people, everyone you enroll after your first line is filled automatically goes under those people. That's called *spillover*.

The positives of a binary plan are that you can make money more quickly because you have upline help. There is lower attrition and a higher reorder rate than with most other plans. If you have a powerhouse above you, this system could work well because of the spillover.

There are also a few negatives. This is a new system, not completely proven. Sometimes people sell the spillover rather than the product. With most binaries, if you have unequal sales volume in two legs, you do not get paid on the sales of your entire organization. (A leg is a group of people in your organization under someone on your front line.)

Table 1.1: The Binary Plan

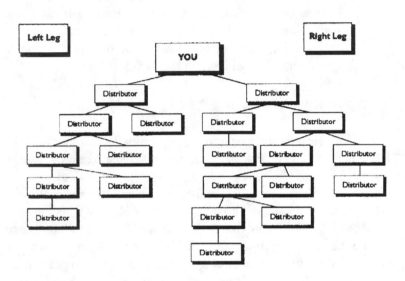

The Expandable Matrix

The third popular system is an expandable matrix program. These plans are not designed to make you quick money, but are designed to produce consistent long-term residual income. Matrix programs allow you to put between four and six people on your front line. This makes it possible for you to go wide enough to have a large customer base, but does not force the stacking or spillover concept upon people.

Expandable matrix programs allow you to go wider on your front line once you reach a leadership level. This allows you to have a downline of unlimited size.

The principal advantage of a good expandable matrix plan, illustrated on page 60, is unlimited *lifetime* income potential. Other advantages are:

1. Many of these types of plans have lasted a long time.
2. Spillover is there, but it's not a big selling point. The *product* is.
1. You are rewarded based on your production. No one you enroll, not even your most aggressive and successful business builders, ever leaves your organization. This means if you enroll someone who does the business faster than you, you do not lose him or her. You keep that business builder and his or her entire organization. If you're a five and enroll a ten, you keep the ten and everyone he or she brings in! The ten does not break away from you! That's a great benefit! You truly are *rewarded for your lifetime*, not only from your own direct efforts but also the efforts of the people you brought into your organization

However, all marketing systems have pros and cons. No plan is perfect, nor is any single plan ideal for everyone.

The negatives of the expandable matrix plan include:

1: People who want to work the business can sometimes be buried under too many customers–people who are satisfied to merely buy the products, but won't become business builders. You need customers in an expandable matrix plan, but without business builders, you won't progress. If you don't bring in and develop business builders, you can, in some cases, become buried under customers who have no interest in the teamwork needed to build your organization.
2: In matrix programs you rarely see people consistently making six figures a month.

The last success factor I'll discuss in this chapter is *timing*.

As I said earlier, a company less than five years old is risky to join because very few networking businesses make it that far.

A company that is over five years old (and meets the other qualifications I've talked about) represents a great opportunity.

59

Expandible Matrix Compensation Plan

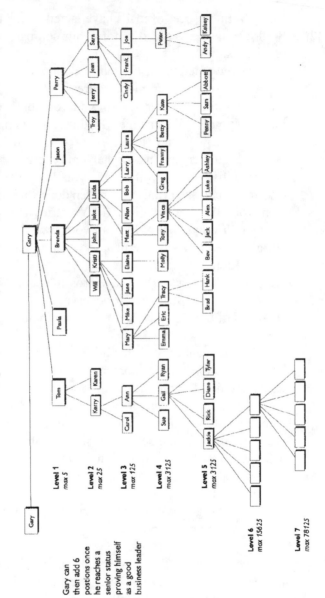

Gary can
then add 6
positions once
he reaches a
senior status
proving himself
as a good
business leader

Level 1
max 5

Level 2
max 25

Level 3
max 125

Level 4
max 3125

Level 5
max 3125

Level 6
max 15625

Level 7
max 78125

I am one of the top income earners in a networking company. I joined it in its seventh year. Myself, and many people under me, have been well rewarded for our choice.

Timing is as important to a networking business as location is to real estate. (You may have heard the real estate expression that the three most important things in real estate are, "Location, location, and location.") Look for a business that is firmly established but youthful enough to support large growth.

In review, it is important to have *all* the success factors discussed in this chapter. If *even one* is missing, your organization, and the time you put into that business, can be at risk in the long run.

You may want to review this chapter and make a personal list of the factors that seem most important to you–but don't leave any of them off your list. I'm not reviewing the success factors here, because I prefer that you look at them again and make your own list of what you feel will be most important to your personal evaluation of a company. Refer to your list as you evaluate each opportunity. It doesn't matter whether you review and make your list now, or whether you make it after you've read the entire book–but *do the review* and *make the list* before you begin the evaluation process.

I hope this chapter has shown you the pitfalls and the benefits of the three most common types of networking companies so you can choose the company that's right *for you.*

It's like a marriage. Marry the wrong person, and suddenly you understand why the divorce rate is over fifty percent! Marrying the *right* person can be beautiful and can last for a lifetime. You want a lasting "marriage" with your network marketing company.

Keep reading! You'll learn how to get started on your road to success in the next chapter.

CHAPTER FOUR

FIRST STEPS: MAKING ALL THE RIGHT MOVES

The first thing you need to do when you start your network marketing business is to be certain you have the right tools of the trade.

Without the tools, you can't start, much less succeed.

It's the same as painters needing paint and brushes before they can paint, musicians needing instruments and music before they can play, or auto mechanics needing screwdrivers and wrenches, etc., before they can fix your car (not to mention the complex electronic testing devices needed today). Every job and profession has its tools. Network marketing is no exception.

If you treat this business as a business, it will pay you like a business.

If you treat this business as a hobby, it will treat you as a hobby–and pay you like one.

You definitely want to treat this business as a business! (If you don't, why bother?)

The Tools of Network Marketing

The first basic, essential tool I recommend is a separate phone line for your business, preferably a business line. A business line costs more than an additional non-business line, but it will get you a listing in the Yellow Pages. Display advertising in the Yellow Pages (which also costs more) can be a major benefit. Even if people aren't looking for you and your products, they may see the display ad while looking for something else and call you.

If your budget is tight, a second, non-business, line will do. It's cheaper, because you're not paying for that business line Yellow Pages listing.

If you're starting on a shoestring, you *can* make your personal line do double duty, but it will cost you business and become a major hassle. You never know whether an incoming call should be answered as a business or personal call, for one thing. One of the many secrets of success is eliminating needless hassles from your business life. Worse than the hassles, however, using the same phone line for personal and business calls shows that you are mixing business with pleasure. *Your business callers will take you less seriously!*

Another secret of success is to be sure that you *always* present a professional business image to everyone you deal with, both in person and on the phone. The telephone part of your professional business image is much easier with a separate business line. Any business line will have a professional business message on your answering machine or voice mail service. It *does not* sound professional if your five-year-old answers your phone when a business call comes through! But if you can only afford one phone line when you begin, and your five-year-old answers sometimes, *that's better than not starting your business at all!* Professional is better, and will build your business faster, but I'm *not* suggesting that you shouldn't start if you can't afford a separate business line in the beginning!

Be sure any service you get provides unlimited outbound calls per month. If that isn't included in your basic service, pay whatever extra is needed for unlimited calls. You'll be doing a lot of calling. The extra fee, whatever it is, will *definitely* cost less than you'd pay for a pay-per-call service!

An example of a phone message that you might want to leave on this line is:

"You have reached the office of Russ Paley. I am currently unavailable, probably because I am on appointments. If you leave your name, phone number with area code, and a brief message I will get back to you within twenty-four hours. Have a profitable day and keep enrolling!"

That's one good example of a professional phone message you might have on your business line answering machine.

You also need three-way calling, call waiting and caller ID.

Three-way calling allows your upline to make conference calls with you when you are setting appointments. When your organization grows, three-way calling makes it simple for you to help the people in your organization to set appointments as they (and you) enroll people and you do three-ways with them. You can call in orders on the spot with new customers. There are many other advantages to three-way calling. It's a *must have!*

The benefits of call waiting are that you can prioritize the importance of calls, you never miss a call, and you have no frustrated people suffering endless busy signals trying to get through to you. You can take a caller's number and call him or her back. You can talk to the people you want to in the order of their importance, and never miss a call.

Caller ID lets you know who the call is from, unless the caller uses the caller ID-blocking feature offered by phone companies. It helps you prioritize calls and may save you the time needed to accept calls from unwanted callers and get rid of them. Even if you get a telemarketing call from, say, one of your credit card companies trying to sell you insurance you don't need (or already have), it takes time to politely tell the person on the other end of the line–who, after all, is trying to make a living in a high-rejection business–that you are not interested, you're busy, and better luck on his or her next call.

Call waiting, caller ID, and conference calling are ideal tools for business line use. Their cost is minimal compared to the benefits.

A good fax machine is an absolute (!!!!) must. A separate fax line is optional (but desirable). As I use the term, "good fax machine," I mean a plain-paper fax machine with *at least* a broadcast fax option. Most have it, but check to be sure before you buy. Such a basic fax machine should cost about $300 with this

64

broadcast option. Prices are dropping. Get the best fax machine you can for the bucks you can spend. *Be sure* to buy a plain paper fax, not one of the old-fashioned thermal paper fax machines. Dealing with slick and curly thermal fax paper is a hassle you don't need. Most fax machines have a copier function which can fill that need until your business grows enough to support a full-sized office copier.

Some fax machines double as computer printers. Many of the current generation of these "Swiss Army" fax machines also print color. For one example, the Hewlett-Packard OfficeJet 500 series, currently about $300, combines plain paper fax, copier, scanner, and prints in both black and white and color! The 600 series, for another hundred bucks or so, also copies in color. That's very useful until you can afford a laser printer, which may cost more to buy, but is usually faster, and *always* costs less per printed page than inkjets–very important if you plan to send out a lot of mailings.

If you need color, however (and color mailers get more attention), inkjet printers are the best choice until your volume of color printing justifies a color laser–they currently start at about $2,500 and go up from there, though color laser prices seem to be dropping.

A computer is useful but optional when you start. When you grow, it will become essential. You can currently buy a very capable computer, with monitor, keyboard, printer for well under $1,000. Companies like Hewlett-Packard and Compaq have systems that come in right around $1,000 with monitor, keyboard and printer. Both companies offer excellent service and tech support. You can find bargains at used computer stores, if there's one in your area, or in the classified ads–but be sure you have any used machine checked out thoroughly before buying! Computer prices keep dropping–check to see what's currently available in your area, on the Internet, or from major mail-order computer companies like Dell and Gateway.

Your fax machine allows you to fax enrollments and customer orders to your company and receive enrollments from others in your organization. (Yes, be sure to recommend that each business builder you enroll buys a fax machine!)

Broadcast fax allows you to send the same information to many people with one keystroke, perhaps to everyone in your organization. You can send important information and announcements to your entire organization by pushing one "send" button.

If your machine can do fax-on-demand, you have one of the most powerful forms of advertising and a great tool for recruiting new customers.

Fax-on-demand works this way: You advertise that people can get more information by calling your fax-on-demand number. People call your fax line and your fax machine automatically faxes them material about your company, describing it in a way that will make people want to look into your opportunity and possibly join your business. Fax-on-demand is there, ready to answer the questions of potential members of your organization twenty-four hours a day. New members can call or fax back enrollment forms.

Your fax machine, especially with fax-on-demand, shows that you're serious about building your business. A fax machine with fax-on-demand capability costs more than a basic machine, but it's worth every penny.

The next basic business tool I recommend is a daily planner.

This is a simple calendar in a small portfolio book which you carry with you at all times. It has one page for each day, with the hours marked on the page and space to write what you will do at any time during each day. Write down the times and dates of your business appointments and training sessions. Confirm your plans for your upcoming week. In addition to obvious benefits, like not promising to be in two places at once, the planner gives you an instant picture of what you are doing, where you need to be and when, and provides you with a record of what you've done in the past (which you can compare to what you achieved, when you review your progress). The planner also tells you what you have lined up in the future. If you look at next week and see that you don't have enough appointments, you know you should get busy and generate more.

Your goals and lists should be in this daily planner as a constant reminder and motivator to keep you focused on the goals you are striving to achieve. It will keep you consistently working on *accomplishment* rather than merely doing *activity* because it will show you exactly what you have done and what you should be doing each week to accomplish your goals.

The planner is a vital record of your activities if you are audited by the IRS. With the planner, you can show documentation of what you did, when, with whom, and why, on a daily basis. Your planner should include a record of your daily expenses for tax purposes. The IRS can be demons about the "contemporaneous record" stuff. You need receipts for expenses, of course, but when you can show them the entries in your planner to back up the receipts, you can go a long way to defuse a hostile inquiry into your expense records. Follow the advice of your tax professional in establishing working practices that don't invite audits, and in setting up record-keeping habits that will satisfy the IRS, if needed. The best time to prepare for an audit is *before* you get the dreaded audit letter–and that's true even if you have a minimum-wage job, not only because you're in business!

Your planner is the best place to keep a record of your referrals and a follow-up list of people you need to contact.

Your daily planner is used again and again to keep you focused on business, a separate part of your life. Like the American Express card ads–*don't leave home without it! And don't let it get away from your phone when you're home!*

Never set an appointment without consulting your planner, and immediately write down every appointment you make.

The next vital thing to do for your business is to dedicate a certain part of your house for business. This is vital both for the business itself and for tax purposes. Costs attributable to a home office are deductible, provided you follow the IRS rules for an "office in home." Check with your tax professional. The basic rule, currently, is that the office in home must be used "exclusively for business." (This is one more reason to have separate business and fax lines going into that room or space.)

Your home office could be a room or part of a room in your home. A full room is much better. You can hold small meetings and one-on-ones in this room. You can set up a product display in this room. Again, it shows your commitment, and that will rub off on people you sign up and help duplicate your efforts within your organization. If you have a home office in a separate room, so will the leaders in your organization. That will come back to help in growing your business. It will also help you develop better organizational skills. You will have everything organized and in one place, not scattered all over your house.

Yes, you can start this business from your kitchen table. Many people have done so. I did–I know it can work! If you *have to* start that small, *start!* But you'll find success is achieved more slowly because you are less organized, will inevitably feel and appear less professional, and will find it harder to do the work you need to do in your office.

The next thing you want to do when setting up your business is to create a full product and service display area in your home, preferably in your home office. This will help you in doing your presentations. It will allow guests who come to see the products an opportunity to get excited about them. It will show your downline that you're product centered. This will increase your average order and your sign-up rate. A picture *really is* worth a thousand words. Visual and physical product contact builds the most successful organizations in this industry.

The next thing you need to do is to have all the products your company sells *visibly* in use in your home. Redirect your spending to these products. ***Take this very seriously!*** Remember, it is not what you *say*, it is what you *do* that people respond to. What *you* do, *they* will do. That's called duplication!

When the products you sell are visible around the house and in obvious use, people will know you believe in and are committed to the products. This can be as simple as making sure that when they use the bathroom–and almost everyone who visits you

68

will–the appropriate products are visible on the sink and in the shower or bath. In your kitchen, make sure the products are visible on the counter-top, not hidden in a cabinet. Visible use of the products increases your believability when you recommend them, and that will increase your sign-up percentage. You can take prospects on a tour of your home, showing them all the products you use and where you use them.

This is like a Mercedes salesman driving a Mercedes, not a BMW or Infiniti or some other car that's in direct competition with the Mercedes. You would rather buy a car from someone who demonstrably believes in the automobile you're buying. (That's why some dealers provide salespeople with company cars.)

You're marketing something that you (and those you sign up) need anyway, so use these products! *Shop from your own store*, rather than shopping from the grocery store. You have to *be a product of the product* to succeed. If you are, you will have higher retention of customers.

Using these basic tools involves minor expenses that will help develop residual income.

Beyond Basic Tools

The next thing I recommend that you do when you start, other than having the basic tools mentioned above, is to have and use an accomplishment sheet.

The accomplishment sheet on the next page is an example of what I mean. This is an example of the accomplishment sheet I use to list exactly what I am doing each day to grow my business.

You need to keep track of how many appointments you have and how many phone calls you make each day. That's what the accomplishment sheet will tell you, so you can see your progress. *Keeping track of your progress is vital!*

Monthly Accomplishment Sheet

Name: _____

Goal For This Month:

    # of New Personal Customers:

    # of New Personal Leaders:

    Total # of New Customers in Organization: _____

ACHIEVEMENTS

Day	Appointments today	New Personal Customers Today	New Group Customers Today	# of Prospecting Calls Made Today
1				
2				
3				
4				
5				
6				
7				
8				
9				
10				
11				
12				
13				
14				
15				
16				
17				
18				
19				
20				
21				
22				
23				
24				
25				
26				
27				
28				
29				
30				
31				

Is it Merely Activity–or Accomplishment?

To be productive in network marketing you must not confuse activity with accomplishment. While you must have activity to accomplish anything, it has to be the *right* kind of activity. Focus on achieving your goals, not on activity for its own sake. As I use the term "activity," it means busy-work–being active for the sake of the activity, not with the intent or possibility of accomplishing your goals.

Activity, alone, will not get you to your goals. Think of a car stuck in a snowbank, spinning its wheels and going nowhere. Lots of activity, no accomplishment. Activities for the sake of being active are time-wasters.

This is not to say that some activities–anything which does not, of itself, *directly* produce business–are not valuable and necessary. Publishing your own newsletter will not, *of itself,* create much business–but it will help establish and maintain the enthusiasm of the people in your organization. Putting out a newsletter, perhaps distributing it via fax, or fax-on-demand or over the Internet, is an activity with a long-term payoff.

Begging people to become business builders, however, is an activity you can spend a lot of time on–and get no results. You cannot drag anybody across the finish line in this business. Begging gets no results, no matter how much activity you devote to it. Who, after all, respects a beggar?

Never beg; always work with the people who are already motivated!

You'll find that motivation takes a lot less time and is a lot more effective!

Accomplishment is doing things that directly help you achieve your goals. Accomplishment creates results. Prospecting, making phone calls, making follow-up calls, setting up appointments, and doing appointments for your organization lead to accomplishment. Use the accomplishment sheet to keep track of what you do for your business.

You can generate a lot of non-productive activity by analyzing the products, materials and other things over and over again. That's a *real* time-waster! Too much analysis causes paralysis.

Setting appointments without confirming them is activity with a high risk of little or no accomplishment. *Confirm all your appointments!*

Trying to give a presentation over the phone is activity without accomplishment. I call that *vomiting over the phone*. (Would you like someone to vomit all over you thorugh the phone? How many telemarketers have you hung up on when they made you feel like that?) You want to create *curiosity* on the phone but not give a *presentation*.

Some people will never join your organization. A common mistake—we all make it until we learn to recognize the symptoms—is trying to bring in someone who just isn't cut out for network marketing, or isn't motivated. If they did join, they'd achieve little and drop out soon. I call this *reactivating the dead*.

Some people persist in believing that reactivating the dead is a better use of their time than recruiting new people. After all, the first contact has been made, some kind of relationship has been established, and there seems to be some possibility that this person can be brought on board and made productive. *That is not true! That's a wishful myth.*

Unless you've had previous marketing experience or are an unusual natural talent, you'll spend some time doing this, in the beginning, until you've worked with enough people to recognize the tell-tale signs. If (when) you do, don't let it bother you. Don't worry about it unless you're still trying to reactivate the dead after a year or so of experience. Everyone does their share of attempting to reactivate the dead; it's a problem only if you don't learn to tell the difference between the dead and the alive.

A far better use of your time is recruiting new people.

As I've said, networking is a numbers game, like everything else. You won't sign up everyone to whom you make a presentation, and everyone who signs up will not be productive.

You're looking for and want to work with people who are live prospects, who will go out and duplicate your efforts.

Chasing people who listen to a presentation and say they aren't interested is another thoroughly useless activity. You might call it exhuming the dead and buried–and grave-robbing is *not* profitable! Avoid thinking that if you just present it a little better they'll be interested. They won't.

Working within the structure of your organization, with prospects who show sincere interest, will produce a profit. Anything else is useless activity.

Now let's look at more forms of accomplishment.

Getting referrals from people is accomplishment.

So is making new contacts at home-based business shows, clubs, at a new job, or through social, business or recreational functions, or anywhere you have the opportunity to make a contact.

Setting up appointments and confirming them the night before is accomplishment, as is creating curiosity and interest until you get an appointment to actually meet the person and give your presentation.

Getting new personal customers or distributors is accomplishment.

Signing up people as business builders or customers on your first few levels is also accomplishment.

Accomplishment is Crucial to Success

When you're getting started, it is crucial to stick to the accomplishment side of this list to move your business forward. It isn't always easy, and most of you will make your share of mistakes. The key to success is to *learn from mistakes*, not let them get you down. To stay focused on those items, post a list of these questions in your office, where you can't avoid looking at them every day. List them in your daily planner as well. These reminders help you keep your focus.

The Five Key Questions

1. How many appointments have I set on the phone today?
2. How many new contacts did I meet and add to my list of prospects?
3. How many referrals did I get from people who did not join my business?
4. How many personal customers did I sign up today?
5. How many appointments did I do for my organization today?

If the answers to these five questions every day or every other day are more than zero, you're on the right track to being in the black in your business and your quest to have a financially independent situation for yourself and your family.

Six Homework Assignments

Once you have the tools and know how to spend your time to assure accomplishment, it is time to do what I call the *Six Homework Assignments* to launch your business.

The *Number One Homework Assignment*, which I tell everybody to do when they join my organization and start doing network marketing, is to thoroughly read *all* the information you received when you joined. Write down any questions or ideas or concerns that you have. The more you dedicate yourself to the products and services, the company's history, the compensation plan, and the way your business operates, the easier it will be to launch your business successfully. Watch or listen to all the tapes that deal with starting your business.

Homework Assignment Number 2:

Write down a contact list. This should include everyone you know, from acquaintances you had five years ago at your old job to your best friend and your parents. Put phone numbers next to every person on your list. If they have second phone lines or work phone numbers, include those number, too. You want to have least two hundred names on your list. *Don't* try to keep the list in your memory or rely on your address book! *Write it down! Make a list!*

After you have a list, if it contains less than one hundred names, get out your Yellow Pages. Go through the directory and expand your list with it.

You're certain to ask, "How do I do that?"

Good question–almost everyone without marketing training and experience will wonder how that can work. Actually, it's simple.

Go through the Yellow Pages and look at the top right-hand corner of each page. You'll see the familiar listings of accountants, actuaries, bookkeepers, carpenters, dog trainers, electricians, all the way to zoologists–the professions and businesses you're used to seeing. There will also be an index of categories with the page numbers where you'll find them. This index will help you think of professional categories you might not have originally thought of as prospects for your list. Look at these professions and businesses and think about what makes people successful in each of them. Which professions are likely to have people who would be interested in the network marketing opportunity you're offering?

When you have a long list of names, divide the list into three categories.

Put a "U" next to people that you think would be users of your products. *User-customers* are people who will buy and use the products, but won't go out and find new people for your organization or theirs. Who might be customers of your product? If you're marketing consumables, necessities or services that people need and use every day, anybody you know is a potential customer of your business.

Then put a "B" next to people you think might be *business builders*. Business builders are people whom you believe need or would like to make extra money. These are entrepreneurs, people who have been successful in some type of business, people you know who have the desire to change their lives, people you know who are in debt, need to pay for college tuition, hate their jobs, want to change their lives financially, etc. These are potential business builders. These are the people you need to build your business.

Put the letter "C" next to people on your "chicken" list. Your *chicken list* includes people you hesitate or are afraid to call, for whatever reason, but whom you know could be absolutely the best people you enroll in your business–*if you just call them!* (Don't let yourself chicken out and not call them!)

This will help you figure out your phone approaches (there are different ways to approach different people with different needs), which you will learn later in this book. For example, you will call someone you expect to become a customer in a different way than you would call a probable business builder. Hence, you won't want to invite a customer the same way. You may want to take a slightly different approach to those on your chicken list, based on your reasons for having that hesitation about calling them. Basically, you should talk to your chicken-list prospects the same way you talk to business builders.

Homework Assignment Number 3:

Have *written* goals. Goals are achievements you want to reach for a reason. (If you have no reason to achieve a goal, why bother achieving it?) The first part of the goal-setting process is to establish the *exact tangible reason (or reasons)* why you are doing this business. *Put that reason or those reasons on paper.* Ask yourself all the questions you can think of about why you want to be in this business. Then identify the reasons which will drive you to accomplish your goals.

Answer these questions, and be very specific about why you are doing this business.

Why are you venturing into this business? What is the number one tangible goal you intend and expect to achieve?

The answer cannot be money.

Money, *for its own sake*, is *never* a sufficient reason or goal!

Be specific. Let's look at some examples of tangible goals. You want to pay off the mortgage. You want to buy a new car. You want to buy a second home. You want to retire early. You want to get out of debt. You want to be financially independent so that you can enjoy spending time more with your family. You don't want to work overtime anymore. You want your spouse to retire and be home with the kids. *You* want to be home with your kids! You want your kids to go to the best colleges. These are tangible goals.

Yes, achieving these goals requires money, but money, by itself, is a **means of achieving the goal,** not the **motivating goal itself.**

These goals are the driving reasons or forces that will keep you motivated and focused on continuing achievement in your business.

The next questions are:

1. How much money do you need?

2. Starting today, how much time and how many years do you expect and intend to devote to acquiring the money you need to achieve your goals?

3. How will your life be different once you achieve your goals?

After you have answered these questions and *written down* a very *specific* reason why you are doing this business, I want you to take a picture of your tangible goal, whether it's a credit card statement because you are trying to get out of debt, the dream house you always wanted, or whatever visually represents the goals you have written down. Post that picture in your office, or somewhere where you will see it every single day.

I want you to remember that, *if you continue to do what you have always been doing,* you will *never get where you want to be.* But if you do something different, like this business, and stay focused on your tangible goals, you absolutely can achieve what you want.

The second goal is an action plan. Like any goal, there are some questions you should ask yourself what you must do to achieve it.

What *specific* actions do you need to take to achieve this goal?

How many personal customers will you enroll in the next thirty days to achieve your tangible goal?

77

How many phone calls or appointments will you make to reach your goal?

How much money do you want to make in the next three months?

How much money would you like to make in the next six months, the next twelve months?

How many presentations do you need to do each week to achieve your goals in three, six, and twelve months?

You see, actions are as important as goals–if they are *planned, productive actions,* not mere *wheel-spinning activity.* That's why calendaring and having a daily planner are so important for keeping you focused on your goals.

Remember, reaching your goals is like a marathon, not a hundred-yard dash. You *don't* have to run this "marathon" in world-record time. Real marathon runners don't–after all, there's only one world record. Dedicated runners, however, have a useful term for their times: *Personal Best.* They constantly strive to improve that personal best time–and they compare their results only with themselves. In networking, the best you've done–so far–is your personal best. Like a runner, always strive to improve *your* personal best. Like runners, you *do* have to take every step needed to reach the finish line. Winners in network marketing are those who move forward toward their goals and never give up.

Another important step in goal-setting is to revise your goals monthly. You want your goals to be realistic, but you also want those goals to push you to a level that is a little bit hard for you to achieve. That makes you work to expand your limits so you are on track to achieving more and more as you gain experience and confidence.

You *definitely* want to have written goals, because *goals that are not written down will not be achieved.* Written goals definitely will have a far better chance of becoming reality. It is not only good to have goals in your home-based business but in anything you want to achieve, whether it's losing weight, getting a raise at work, or finishing school.

A Goal Is Hollow Without an Action Plan

When you work with the accomplishment sheet I provided earlier, you will realize that your *attitude* determines your *altitude* in anything you do–you'll never reach higher than your attitude!

Setting Goals

"He who aims at nothing is sure to hit it!"

1. Fix in your mind exactly what it is you desire. It is not sufficient merely to say "I want plenty of money". Be definite as to what it is you want.

2. Determine exactly what you intend to give in return for what ever it is you desire. (There is no such reality as "something for nothing".)

3. Establish a definite date when you intend to possess what ever it is you desire.

4. Create a definite plan for carrying out your desire, and begin at once, whether you are ready or not, to put this plan into action

5. Write out a clear, concise statement of what ever it is you plan to acquire, name the limit for its acquisition, state what you intend to give in return for it, and describe clearly the plan through which you intend to acquire it.

6. Read your written statement aloud twice daily. Once just before retiring at night, and once after arising in the morning. As you read -- see, feel, and believe yourself already in posession of whatever it is you desire.

Excerpts above from:
"Think and Grow Rich," by Napoleon Hill,
'Six Steps that Turn Desires into Gold'

You have to *believe* you will achieve your goals. *(If you believe you can't–you're right!)* Negative thought guarantees a negative result. Positive affirmations help you. *(If you believe you can, you will!)* The concept of underestimating and over-delivering or over-achieving helps. I see many people set what I feel are *unrealistic goals* for themselves. *That's a guarantee of failure.* If you set goals too high and don't reach them, you can't help feeling like you've failed, right? If that happens to you, take another look at the goals and see whether they were, in fact, realistic. Adjust your goals to something you believe you can achieve, and try again.

Unrealistic goals are a major reason why networkers give up. It is better to be conservative and over-achieve your goals.

Homework Assignment Number 4:

Once you've established and set your goals, and identified the actions that clearly define what it will take to reach them, the next critical step in getting started is to set your *store hours*. Store hours are the exact times and days you commit to building your customer base. Mark those hours in your planner and on your calendar. If you need a larger reminder, make a large chart showing your store hours and put it up in your office where you will see it every day.

I want to make a couple of clear statements, up-front.

You will not be successful doing any business in your *spare* time, which is defined as whenever you get around to it.

If you treat this as a business, it will reward you as a business.

You can, however, be very successful in your *part* time even if it is as little as a few hours a week–provided you commit to work those hours at specific times.

This will require some sacrifice. To achieve your goals, you will have to give up one or more of the activities that now fill your time. After all, you *do* fill up your time now. How many of us have a few unused hours in the day, just lying around waiting for us to use for network marketing or anything else? If you add an activity to your day, you have to *make* time for it, not *take* time. *Taking time* is doing something when you get around to it; when you find some time you can take. *Making time* is establishing your store hours, blocking out the time when you will work and allowing

80

nothing to interfere–perhaps short of a child's illness or other extraordinary reason. You *make* the time available.

Making time usually involves deciding what you will no longer do.

What will you give up? It's different for everyone, of course, but maybe you could do without watching re-runs on TV, going to your bowling league, or your guys (or girls) night out, watching your soap operas, working on your knitting, watching a movie, or being a couch potato after work. Sacrifice a couple of unproductive activities and you open the way to accomplishment in your business.

Learning Curve Graph

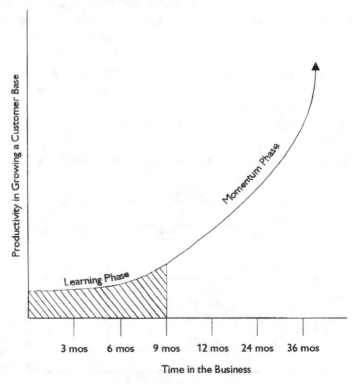

In a few years you will be able to go back to those activities–if you still want to–after you reach the goals you set for yourself, because you'll have the money to enjoy those goals and that lifestyle.

You should expect to spend more time during the first six months than you will later on. Your initial learning curve (see graph on previous page) will take more time. It's that simple. You have to take the time to learn, to develop your skills, to make, recognize, and understand your mistakes and learn from them, and become an accomplished professional network marketer.

As you will see, going to training sessions, listening or watching tapes, and signing up new customers will be time-consuming at first, but will become second nature after enough repetition. You'll always be learning new techniques, but when you first start to learn these products and services, the compensation plans and the enrollment process, it will take more time because it will be foreign to you. If you devote the time needed to learn these success principles for your business, they will serve you well. You'll find it much easier to learn new or refined techniques and methods later.

Do this week by week. This is also called calendaring. Setting

Calendaring the Hours You Will Work Your Business is so Crucial

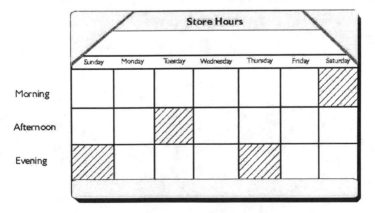

store hours is critical to staying disciplined and focused on your goals.

It's just like going to the gym. Those who care about their bodies and their health go to the gym consistently. They have set, planned hours for when they go to the gym each week, just as you probably work consistent hours at your regular job. You work for your employer forty or more hours each week in order to get ahead. Those are the "store hours" your employer sets and demands of you. In your business, you are your own employer. Set store hours and demand them of yourself.

Homework Assignment Number Five:

Go to an opportunity presentation or a training session in your area sponsored by your upline or the company. An opportunity presentation, open enrollment meeting, or business presentation usually takes one or two hours. It's a great vehicle for enrolling new customers and creating interest in potential customers.

I believe that as a new business builder it is a good idea for you to go to one or two of these meetings to observe how a seasoned person does the presentation and close.

Go to training sessions to learn the business from experienced people who have been a part of it longer. You will meet people who are already successful in your business. This will allow you to ask questions and get them answered. It will also pump up your believability factor, which will help you sign up a higher percentage of the people you contact because you will have more enthusiasm, and your own beliefs and enthusiasm will rub off on them.

Remember, your attitude determines the quality of the results in your business. Success breeds success. If you want to be a successful accountant, then in the beginning you want to work with people who are also successful accountants.

Applying the principles you learn at training sessions will make the path to creating your business smooth from the beginning. Instead of a trial and error approach, you'll learn what's been proven to work and what doesn't. You don't want to re-invent the wheel. Take all the ideas and strategies you learn and apply the ones that fit you best. By going to training meetings, you'll be able to team up with other people in your area who have similar goals and ambitions. This is especially critical if your sponsor is out of town or not active. Go up to the person doing the training and get your questions answered.

The people who are now my best leaders were like sponges for information. They'd follow me out to the parking lot after meetings and drive through snowstorms to get to the presentations. Those are the people who are making the most money in my business today.

The Sixth Homework Assignment:

To start your business, meet with the most successful people in your upline who will grant you a few hours of their time. Do the first five Homework Assignments before setting the appointment for this meeting.

Before this meeting, accomplish the following start-up steps:

(1) Set up the presentation book you will use to enroll future customers. Have the leader show you how he or she does a one-on-one presentation or a small group meeting. The leaders, after all, have proven that what they do works, or they would not be leaders. They're happy to share their knowledge, because they want you to succeed, too. Take notes on the appropriate pages you will use during your presentation. These are called cheat sheets and are like training wheels on a bicycle. Eventually they come off, once you can ride without falling. They remind you what to do and say at any given point.

(2) Ask your leader all the vital questions you have. Make a list, to be sure you don't forget to ask anything. Be sure you understand the products and the compensation plan. Be sure you get all the basic information you need to know to get started.

(3) Spend enough time to learn how to prospect, invite, and overcome objections. Write down several key phrases or sentences you like that you think will increase your chance of setting an appointment. Role play back and forth with the leader so that you will be prospecting him or her, and he or she will be prospecting you. Practice makes perfect in this area! There's nothing like doing

84

it over and over again! Write down all future training and opportunity presentations in your area on a calendar or in your planner so you can let your future enrollees know about upcoming events.

Try to get some time with the leader, or someone that he or she refers you to, to help you go out and do some two-on-one presentations. Two-on-one presentations are where you and the more experienced upline person go to someone's home or office and present the business, with both of you presenting to this new person. This will help you learn how to do the presentation effectively and see more immediate success.

If your leader cannot go with you, see whether there is a company video that's sufficient to teach you how to present the opportunity the first times you do it. Ask to be included in any voice-mail system, mailing list or other systems your upline people and your sponsor use to communicate within their organizations. The more communication you have with successful people and the more success you are exposed to, the better.

Photocopy your goal sheet and give your leader a copy. Ask, "Put yourself in my shoes starting out. What should I do each week to achieve the goals that I just gave you?"

Their answers will tell you the activities you must perform to lead you to accomplish what you desire. Ask your leader what it will take for you to become successful. Have him or her write down the top ten things they do each week to build their organization to the level of success he or she had achieved. If you duplicate successful people in your marketing company, you will become equally successful.

CHAPTER FIVE:

THE ART OF SEDUCTION: CATCHING FLIES WITH HONEY *OR* VINEGAR

Prospecting can take many forms. Many of them will be covered in this chapter, followed by detailed scripts of how to invite your prospects.

The most popular and successful form of prospecting to start your business is to begin with people you know. These prospects are called *warm list people*.

After you write down the names and phone numbers of your prospects for this memory jogger list, get out your Rolodex, any other new or old address books you may have, old yearbooks, wedding invitation lists, and your Yellow Pages.

Go through the Yellow Pages and look at the kinds of businesses and professions listed in bold type words at the top of each page. It will help you remember people in every profession, from accountants to zoologists–people who are missing from your warm list. If you know a zoologist, this exercise will help you remember that person, whom you might have left out.

Remember: prospecting, using this list, is the road map to your success.

If someone paid you $100 for each name and phone number you put on your prospect list, how many would be on your list? Well, over time your business will pay you residuals that could far exceed $100 for every person on your list. Remember: If you prejudge or forget someone, that person could make someone else wealthy and not be in your organization.

Once you complete your warm list, start calling these people. There are good reasons to call them first.

The first benefit: You'll have less rejection. People on your warm list will be more willing to talk to you, because they know you. For the same reason, they'll be more likely to listen and respond, even if your presentation is still less than perfect or a bit unpolished.

The second benefit: You'll have more immediate success because warm list people will feel you are their friend or relative. They'll give you more time, and you'll have more success enrolling them.

The third benefit: What you are doing is duplicatable. What *you* are doing, *others* will do. You want your new people to start with their own warm lists.

87

Setting an example for your organization is very important. If *you* don't do it, you can't expect *them* to do it.

The fourth benefit: You will create your lukewarm list from referrals from people who don't want to enroll. When a prospect decides not to join your organization, never forget to ask whether he or she knows others who might be interested.

The fifth benefit: There are no large expenses during your learning curve.

If you're in a really great business, don't you owe it to the people you know to offer them the opportunity to benefit as well? Your credibility and friendship will also give you a higher percentage sign-up rate.

The sixth benefit: You can use the opinion approach which is an excellent, low-rejection way to get appointments.

A good example of the opinion approach is:

"Mary, I've always respected you as a businesswoman for the success you've achieved as both a professional and a mother. I was recently shown a business that I think is quite lucrative. I'd greatly appreciate it if you could give me your expert opinion on this business. Can you spend a lunch hour with me this week?"

Complimenting someone, as in the script above, is the best route to success in the opinion approach–but the compliment must be honest and fully justified or it becomes mere flattery. Flattery, as has been said over and over, will get you nowhere, save with those too dumb to spot it–with whom, as the opposite saying goes–flattery will get you everywhere. But do you want to go there, with that kind of person? The kind of successful businessperson you want to recruit to become a business leader in your organization got where they are by, among other skills, learning to spot flattery a mile away.

Use the opinion approach only on successful business people you respect, whom you think wouldn't normally give you an appointment. (Offering them a free lunch certainly will help.)

After You Contact Everyone on Your Warm List

After you have reached or attempted to reach every person on your warm prospecting list–and when I say "reached" I mean actually talked to or met with–the next step in the art of prospecting is getting referrals from those who say, "No, thanks, I'm not interesting in meeting with you. This is not my kind of opportunity."

Your goal in prospecting is to never run out of names on your list. The best way to assure that you never run out of names is to add two to four referrals for every person on your warm list who doesn't want to meet with you.

Now, let's be frank. Not everyone who says no to you will give you referrals. That's why you want to get more than one referral from everyone who says no, but will give you referrals.

Never forget that prospecting is a numbers game!

Prospecting is a Numbers Game

As you get more experienced on the phone
your percentages will get better
but as a new networker you can expect

100   Phone Calls Attempted

50   You will reach in any given evening

25   You will make an appointment with

This is called the (4) Phone Calls = (2) you will reach
= (1) You will secure an appointment with
(or the 4-2-1 method)

Nobody gets everyone they call–I don't; you won't. Not everyone who joins your organization will become a business builder–not even those who appear to be naturals. Reality in networking is that you have to keep prospecting to find the people who will seize the opportunity you offer and take off and run with it.

It *doesn't matter* how many prospects you must call to find people who will become business builders.

What matters is that you keep prospecting and *find those people.*

And, just as some people who appear to be naturals for networking never do anything, you'll also find those you think will never be more than a customer who suddenly realize that *I can do this (!!!!)* and prosper with the opportunity. It can be as amazing as Clark Kent stepping into a phone booth and emerging as Superman. There's nothing more rewarding in networking than seeing someone make that kind of life-change to success!

The people who give you referrals will keep your list growing rather than shrinking.

How do you get referrals?

Here are a few good ways.

When a friend or family member doesn't want to meet with you, or says no after your presentation, say, "I totally respect and understand your position, but it would be a great favor if you could provide me the names of a few sales, marketing, or network marketing people whom you know who might be interested in getting together with me for mutual gain in this opportunity. People like your insurance agent, your Realtor, Tupperware marketers or your Mary Kay lady. Can you put me on hold so you can get those names and numbers? It would really be helpful to me, and I would owe you a big favor."

If they say no to that, ask them one more time for referrals, explaining to them that you guarantee you will not use their names in the call. That might be their concern. You *don't* want to have your contact call their referrals. *You* want to.

I call this referral list the *lukewarm list*. The longer you can invite warm and lukewarm contacts, the higher your batting average will be and the lower your rejection rate will also be.

Remember, rejection is one of the biggest reasons why people stop working the business. Look for ways to avoid rejection, find every way you can to increase your success rate, but do not, *ever*, let rejection discourage you. Remember that old saw about "sticks and stones may break my bones, but words can never hurt me?" The word "no" can never hurt you–unless you let it. The only meaning "no" has for you is, "Okay, so much for this prospect. Now let's get on to the next one on my list!"

Other Prospecting Techniques

Other forms of prospecting are additional or supplemental methods to be used in conjunction with the basic method described above. These techniques should become part of your prospecting arsenal some months after your date of enrollment with your networking company, after you have given your presentation many times, begun to build your organization, and polished your skills. They should never take precedence over prospecting your warm and lukewarm contacts. Use these techniques as *additional*, not *primary*, prospecting methods.

The first of these prospecting methods is to place ads in local or area newspapers or in magazines. When I started, I ran ads seeking to drum up some good prospects. Here are examples of a couple of generic ads you could run for your company.

Example 1: Explosive marketing company is entering this area! If you would like to earn an extra $3,000 to $5,000, part-time, or a full-time $10,000 a month residual income with no selling, inventory, delivery or cold calling, call me at (your phone number) for more information.

Example 2: Are you sick of the rat race? I work with a company that has helped thousands supplement their income. Some have been able to fire their boss! Call (your phone number) to hear a 30 second recorded announcement about an opportunity that could change your life forever.

Example 3: If you continue to do what you have always done in the past to earn money, your future results will be the same. If you are ready for a part-time change, with little investment, and want to own your own business, call me at (your phone number).

Example 4: Drive your dream car. Live in a beautiful home. Retire early. Pay off your debt. My company is making these dreams a reality for reps in a business with unlimited potential and no downside risk. Call me at (your phone number) for more information and to set up an appointment.

The advantages of newspaper ads are:

(1) They target many thousands of people whom you normally would not know or have any way to contact.

(2) You may find and contact someone very influential or in a different target market with whom you would not normally make connections. Remember, one of the keys to fast success for you and your organization is to recruit up. These ads might help you get someone who normally would not be on your list. Your list is primarily people whose age, gender, interests, and religious and economic backgrounds are similar to yours. Sometimes that can be a disadvantage, especially if you're young or don't have many business-like friends or colleagues.

(3) You can start in an area you want to build up without personally knowing anybody there. If I'm going to be at a meeting in Dallas, I place a few ads in a Dallas paper before I get there. The ads include an 800 number with a recorded announcement designed to screen out the non-serious interested parties from those who are seriously interested. Then I make some personal, one-on-

one appointments in that area, based on the most promising responses to my 800 number message.

Some disadvantages of placing ads are:

(1) They cost money. You will have a cash outlay ranging from a few dollars to several thousand dollars a week, depending on the paper's circulation, the size of the ad, and the area where you are placing the ad. Try to discount the ad's cost by doing a multi-week ad. That means your ad is in the paper every day for weeks at a time–and repetition is necessary for advertising success. Most newspapers offer discounts per appearance of an ad if you run it more that once, more than a week, etc. Ask the advertising department what it offers and what it can do for you.

Experts say that to grow a business you should expect to put some of your profits back into your business to increase your future profits; that you "...have to spend money to make money." I agree, though networking costs are much less than they're talking about. I believe you should not spend more than five percent of your income on general, un-targeted, marketing of any kind. Only seasoned veterans, who really know how to handle the cold market, should place ads at all.

(2) There is a high amount of rejection.

(3) There is no trust or relationship between you and the person who responds to the advertisement. Thus, the percentage who will actually meet with you for an appointment will be much lower than from your lukewarm or warm list.

(4) Most respondents to these types of ads are looking for a job. You want to make it clear in your ad that it *isn't* a salaried position and it is *not* a job. You'll still get calls from job-seekers who don't read what your ad actually said, but you won't get as many.

Despite these disadvantages, ads can be a good way to prospect successfully. I recommend that you follow these guidelines:

To lower costs, co-op with people in your group and split the follow-up on the resulting leads based on who is closest, geographically, to that specific person.

93

Place an ad that is within your budget–and *test, test, test, and test more*. Different papers, different ads, days, weekends. Try everything; test everything.

To be successful, you want to make sure that you test your marketing (ads, letters, phone calls and all other techniques) to get the best results possible. In the case of newspaper advertising, stop placing any ad that doesn't result in an instant breakeven situation. If your first few sign-ups from responses to the ad cannot cover the up-front costs of the ad, it might not have been a successful thing to do.

Be smart in your business. If your investment in any form of marketing is consistently greater than your profits, stop using that part of your marketing repertoire. Keep track of the costs and responses to each marketing technique you try.

Keep to a small, conservative ad at first, until you learn which newspaper gives the best response, and learn which day is best to run it. Do trial and error the most inexpensive way. Negotiate the best package deal you can get with a newspaper. Some deals will allow you to place an ad in multiple newspapers for one price, if one company owns and operates many different papers.

Underestimate and over-deliver.

Don't place untrue ads to entice people to call. Aside from considerations of attracting highly negative attention from you state's Attorney General and others, this will cause animosity down the road–if not almost instantly.

Never forget that bad word-of-mouth spreads faster than good!

Anything misleading will cause problems *right away* with appointments you set. You'll be meeting with people who expect more than you can offer. They'll say no. You want to minimize rejection, remember! This is not the way to build a successful relationship with your future business builders. That relationship is *critical* in network marketing! The last thing you want to do is undermine your relationship with your current or potential partners, the business builders who are so critical in networking.

Another form of prospecting which has had some success for many networkers is going to home-based business shows and conventions. Membership (preferably active) in business clubs and organizations can be quite productive. Networking is the art of meeting people with the intent to match a product or service with the needs of an individual. Many who attend conventions and business shows are there for one reason: To look for ways to earn extra money. A great approach is to take several people who are part of your organization with you to the show. Make sure you and everyone you bring looks sharp and has plenty of business cards. Walk around the expo, be on the lookout for likely prospects, and talk to them. What that means is to be friendly, make eye contact, introduce yourself and say, "Hi, my name is Russ. Have you found anything interesting?"

No matter how the person responds, say, "Really, well, I think I've found a business you might be great at. If you want, I could take your number and call you about it after the show is over since we're both too busy here trying to gather information from what this show has to offer. Would you like me to do that for you?" If the prospect starts asking questions, say, "I really need an hour to explain everything. I can't do the business justice standing here right now, but I promise I'll call you tomorrow to set up an appointment to give you all the details. What time is best for me to call you tomorrow?"

The advantages of this approach are:

(1) It costs little or no money, other than travel to the event, perhaps lunch or dinner, and your business cards. It costs time, of course, but the time is productive prospecting time.

(2) You will learn a lot about your competition, as well as learning about other business concepts.

(3) The people who go to these expos are looking for opportunities, so they are already pre-qualified.

(4) They are mainly business people. These are exactly the kind of people who can contribute to major growth in your business.

There are a few disadvantages, though.

95

The first disadvantage is that if you *openly* prospect at these shows, you might be asked to leave. It could create great embarrassment for you. That's why you want to quickly get the name and number, hand out the business card, and move on.

The second disadvantage is that you're meeting people cold. That makes for a high rejection level, even among prospects who are looking for an opportunity and have the skills to take off and run with it. They may not be interested in *your* opportunity. You have a credibility gap problem because they've never met you and don't know you. That can result in a lot of rejection, right there on the floor, before you get the first name and phone number or set the first meeting. (As always, ignore rejection and go on to the next prospect.)

Overall, in spite of the disadvantages, this is a great method for getting new potential business builders in your organization, especially if you are an extrovert and have no problem talking to strangers.

Using Modern Technology to Prospect and Work with Your Organization

Don't ignore the Internet, and other new technology, when you look for new customers and business builders.

The Internet offers an effective way to prospect. You can get lists of e-mail addresses and do a mass e-mailing, advertising your business and providing a phone number that recipients can call if they want more information. If you have a Web site, the e-mail can direct recipients to go there for more information.

Your Web site should provide information about your opportunity, include a FAQ (Frequently Asked Questions) page, and an e-mail response page. Your Web site should also provide the 800 number which interested people can call to request further information, an in-person call-back from you or someone in your organization, which gives you the opportunity to set an appointment.

I recommend Internet marketing for only two types of people: those who have a good knowledge of computers, or already have a Web site for some other business. If you have those qualifications, you know what you're doing. If you don't know what you're doing, Internet marketing can be a vastly unproductive money-drain.

If you lack computer knowledge and skills, I suggest you remedy the situation. Computers and the Internet are the present and future of business, even the smallest business.

Internet marketing–mass e-mailings in combination with a good, well-marketed Web site–can get you lots of leads for potential prospects. I recommend this method when you have a nationwide organization in place to handle these leads. You need to have people who can handle inquiries from anywhere in the nation, or you need contact with others in your networking company who might have someone who could meet a prospect in East Bear Tooth, Montana, when the closest person in your organization is in Salt Lake City.

We'll probably see Internet/e-mail teleconferencing within a few years, when most computers have live video capability. Currently, this is mostly a corporate tool which needs a high-speed Internet connection to work satisfactorily. For the technically-minded among you, that means at least a good cable or DSL service, preferably (as I write) a T-1 or T-3 connection. The latter two are expensive corporate communications tools, but DSL is showing real promise.

A friend tried this with current–early 1999–technology. When asked how it went, he said, "Don't ask!" He explained that when his students came on-line, it seemed that they overloaded the system and nothing worked. But he's a pioneer–he's going to try again after seeing whether he can sort out the technological issues with the service provider! People like my friend are the ones who will make computer teleconferencing a reality for all of us. It will just take some time to become commonplace, like anything else in computer innovation.

Designing and maintaining a Web site can be expensive. It normally requires at least a few thousand dollars to start plus monthly maintenance charges, and it's time consuming. Unless you and your organization can handle most of the leads that come in, this method won't be used to maximum capacity. Once set up, however, a Web site is the most cost-effective way to get good leads.

Before you use any of these prospecting techniques, make sure that you thoroughly read your company's policies and procedures. Don't forget that these have been drawn up by the company's legal department, to protect them–and to protect you! Comply with company guidelines at all times! Many companies won't allow you to use the name of that company in these types of prospecting methods, or by any method not approved by the company. This is a matter of their legal departments wishing to assure that no representative in the field makes public claims contrary to company policy, or exceeds what the company can deliver. Word-of-mouth, one-on-one in small groups is usually the preferred introduction.

Using the Internet is not for beginners. It becomes effective when you've built your organization and perhaps have networked with other top people working with your networking company to assure the broadest possible coverage for Internet responses.

The Internet will make network marketing even more powerful in the 21st century. When the industry began, the telephone was the only form of instant communication. The advent of fax machines, conference calling, and computers in the 1970's and 1980's helped our industry very significantly. These technologies lowered the cost of getting information from one place and person to another and sped up the time needed to get this information out to the public.

Network marketing is a business that relies heavily on communication, so every advance in communication technology has a positive effect on our bottom line. These advances have made network marketing an international business moving billions of dollars of products and services each year.

In the 1990's, fax-on-demand, pre-recorded conference calling, cellular phones, and portable computers have become more popular, less expensive, and faster than ever, greatly aiding the growth of network marketing.

All these advancements *combined* don't equal the impact the Internet is having on the networking industry, and will continue to have in the 21st century.

How to Use the Internet to Get Customers

The Internet offers four basic tools
1: Mass e-mail advertising
2: Communication within your existing organization
3: The Web site of the networking company
4: Your personal Web site

The Internet's first major benefit for our industry is mass e-mail marketing.

A *targeted* mass e-mailing to prospects sends your message to 1,000, 10,000, or even 100,000 or more people who have an e-mail address, with one click on the "send" button of your e-mail program. (Of course you have to set up the e-mail list and prepare your message first.) Your e-mail message markets your products and/or business opportunity. But please note my emphasis on *"targeted."* It's wasteful to send marketing material to people who are unlikely to be interested, and on the Internet the shotgun approach to e-mail marketing becomes spam. As I discuss below, you *do not* want to be guilty of sending spam!

You can do directory searches to create your targeted e-mail list (just as you would target any other list), use your existing mailing lists (which are already inherently targeted), or hire an Internet company to do it for you. When you do this kind of mass e-mailing, you are targeting people in occupations you believe are most likely to produce business builders.

The benefits are simple. It costs much less to reach potential customers than if you do conventional direct mail, radio, or TV advertising. You can get your message to as many people as you want, instantly.

A word of caution, however: Even if you don't now have e-mail or even own a computer (yes, I want you to have both!!!!) you've certainly heard the term, "spam." The last thing you want to do is become known as a spammer.

What is spam? Spam is e-mail the recipient didn't ask for and doesn't want to receive. Spam has become one of the true demon-words of the Internet. How do you send a mass e-mailing without being guilty of spamming? It's simple.

First, target your e-mailing list to people you have good reason to believe will be interested.

Second, include a line in the message (it's usually placed at the end of the message) advising the recipient that if he or she doesn't want to receive more e-mail on this subject from you, he or she can be removed from your list by sending an e-mail message with a specific message to a certain address, and they will be removed from the list. The reason to specify the removal message is that your Webmaster can automate your system to recognize that specific text and automatically remove the person who sends it from your list. If your Web site or e-mail is not yet up to that level of technological sophistication, it makes it much easier to recognize a "Remove me!" message, which might otherwise be a lengthy diatribe by someone who was offended. You certainly don't want to offend anyone or waste time or space on your e-mailing list on people who feel sufficiently negative about your message to take the time to ask that they be removed from your list!

With that sole caution, the greatest benefit of e-mail marketing is that people who have e-mail capability currently tend to be more affluent than average. They are more likely to have money to start a business than a person who doesn't have a computer. They're more likely to be interested in the opportunity you're offering.

A prospective customer can immediately go to a Web site for more information, which speeds up the education process. As I've said, the Web site can be a company site, your personal site, or both. I recommend both.

The Internet is a great tool for expanding your organization all over the world, not just in your town or area.

There are some obvious disadvantages to this approach, however. You need a lot of follow-up to get most of the interested parties to sign up. There is no trust or bond between the two of you since you've never met face-to-face. Because networking is a people business, your sign-up rate will be 1 in 1,000 e-mails–if you're lucky–but 1,000 e-mailed messages are a lot faster and cheaper than marketing that uses conventional methods to reach people.

In most cases, you will get better results, faster, if you go to one of the companies which specialize in creating Internet e-mailing lists. They know how to target your market, how to handle "unsubscribe" requests (a process they can usually automate, saving time and money), and how to assure that you're doing good marketing, not sending spam. (And spam, after all, is *at least as unproductive for you* as it is *annoying* to recipients who don't want it.)

The second main benefit of the Internet is ease of communication, whether you're communicating within your existing organization or marketing prospective new customers and business builders.

Mass e-mailing within your organization (I always urge my business builders to get e-mail) is the fastest and cheapest way to reach people instantly.

Regular mail moves at a snail's pace in comparison and costs much more.

Phone contact, while vital in its own right, is not as efficient as e-mail. Personal contact is important, but isn't needed all the time. Phone contact requires more time to place each call, and you have long-distance charges when you call anyone outside your local calling area.

With a mass e-mailing, you write the message once and send it to your entire organization's e-mailing list with a keystroke. You don't have additional charges. You save a huge amount of time.

You can e-mail a single person, members of a selected group who will be interested in attending a meeting you're giving in their area, or your entire organization.

When I want to promote a meeting, wherever it may be, I e-mail every business builder in that area to let them know about my visit well before the meeting date so they can put the date and time on their calendars. I used to hire an assistant to make long-distance calls to those business builders, one by one. That cost me long-distance charges and the salary of the person making the calls–and it took time to put the list together.

For example, I have a group called "DC Metro area." Every time I do a meeting in that part of the country, I e-mail an announcement to the group three weeks prior to the meeting to spread the word.

I collect e-mail addresses at every function I attend and every presentation I make. I update the list frequently. I check the status of the e-mail and take people off this list who delete their e-mail from me without reading it. I add new business builders to my e-mail list. America Online offers a way to tell whether your e-mail has been deleted un-read. This is an advantage over, for example, direct mail, where you have no way to tell whether the person who got your letter read it or trashed it unopened.

The key is to send the e-mail with a feature called BCC, or blind copied, so people who get this e-mail don't know who else you sent it to. That preserves the privacy of other people's e-mail addresses, which is very important. If someone who gets your e-mail decides to join another networking opportunity, this prevents him or her from using your e-mailing list.

The second way I use the Internet to communicate with my organization is to broadcast new product/service information and compensation plan enhancements. I send this e-mail announcement to my entire business. My monthly online newsletter is sent out electronically, which saves tremendous production and mailing costs. It's just as effective as if it went through the regular mail–and maybe even more so. I can send word about a new product to many thousands of people–and send it the day I learn about it. I do this by having a general list of active marketers, called, "All Business Leaders."

When a generic announcement goes out, it is sent to both business builders and customers.

I use the Internet to organize leadership meetings. I e-mail to a group called "Leaders." This group consists of all the people I've worked with and mentored to a substantial level in the compensation plan. I need to talk to this group, once a month or so, to let them know key leadership issues and get feedback from them. This gives me the opportunity to plan events which will be helpful to them and solidifies communication within the organization.

I use AOL as my Internet provider, and have found it to be very productive in creating business lists to broadcast a message to the right readers.

E-mail is a great way to let members of your organization ask you questions. I'm in touch with as many key people in my business as possible, in person and on the phone, but when you have a large organization all over the country or even the world, there isn't enough time in the day to talk to every one of them. For that reason, I encourage anyone in my business to e-mail me with ideas, potential strategies, and their questions and concerns. With my laptop computer and e-mail, I can respond from anywhere in the nation or world, quickly, at almost no cost, and in very little time.

If you're a business traveler, I strongly recommend that you get a laptop computer for this purpose.

The Internet is far from the only use for your computer. Easy-to-use programs allow you to make and keep your schedule, have an alarm go off to remind you of something, keep your tax deductible bills and receipts in order, and keep track of and update important statistics about your business. These benefits allow your planning and accounting to be fine-tuned to max out every minute you spend and every dollar you earn in your networking business.

The third way I use the Internet is through a Web site created by the networking company I work with. You might not be with a networking company that has this, especially if your company is fairly young, but I would strongly recommend you either create one or convince the company you are with to get with the 21st century way of doing business–*as soon as possible!*

In any case, once you have a company Web site to use, you have many benefits at your disposal. I tell all those I sign up who have computers go to the Web site as soon as they enroll to learn more about the company they've joined. This gives instant credibility to the company and provides a quick, on-line education for the new person. Those are two key factors which help get them off to a good start.

I order my products, sign up new customers, and check on certain key data through the Web site. This saves me time. It's easy to print out invoice numbers and get written receipts for transactions this way.

If your networking company allows it and provides the facilities, you can do a mass e-mailing to many thousands of potential business builders, telling them to go to your company's Web site. You will interest some people in joining before you actually call or meet them.

Your company's Web site might enable you to talk to the corporate management team, get information faxed to you or prospective marketers, receive new product updates, get your client downline sent to you, have a small voice-activated company history available (for those with the ability to access it), and give you and your organization a good picture of the business and product opportunity your business offers.

I want to emphasize that these ways of using the Internet shouldn't be a substitute for the hands-on, face-to-face work needed to build your business. The Internet should be used as an *additional* approach to marketing, and a *massive* way to communicate, but not the only way.

Networking will always be a people and a relationship building business.

Trade Shows and Expos

Another effective prospecting method is to set up your own booth at a trade show, flea market, or at home-based business or health expos. Remember to get approval from your company before spending cash to buy space or a booth at one of these functions. The advantage is that it allows you to meet face to face with many interesting people who are looking for an opportunity, and whom you would not normally meet. Here are some tips for setting up a successful booth at one of these functions.

Co-op with the right people. You need to have strong, experienced people, with good, out-going personalities, to work a booth like this. Remember, you probably have thirty seconds or less to impress a potential customer–to give them a reason to keep talking to you. Remember that they will see a lot of other booths. Make your booth unique and memorable so when you call visitors to set up an appointment they will remember you.

Have a raffle. There will be a lot of people to whom you just won't be able to give quality time, but if you raffle something, it will prompt them to fill out a small questionnaire card that you can later use to call them back and follow up the contact.

Have a VCR and TV showing a video about your company and its products. This is an eye-catcher to grab peoples' attention. It will help you compete with nearby booths and will interest people in your program. (The bigger your TV screen, the better!) It's another tool in your campaign to interest people.

Have an attractive person give out sample literature and products. You want a man or woman who is good-looking, personable, and comfortable about meeting and talking with strangers. If you or your assistants see someone who looks sharp and professional, try to get his or her business card. Spend time with *quality people*, not *quantities* of people. Yes, prospecting is a numbers game, but out of the numbers you want that *one* business builder. Remember, one good prospect could ignite your entire business. You can find *customers* anywhere. There's nothing wrong with customers–you need them–but the purpose of having a booth is to find and recruit *potential business builders* who might not normally be on your list.

Have a complete and professional product display. This will give someone a good idea of what might interest them about your company. The more you have to offer, the greater your variety of products and services, the better your chances of appealing to large numbers of people. (And while looking for business builders, don't overlook potential customers!)

If at all possible, book your booth early so you can get a good location in the busiest part of the exhibition hall. You want a place where most people will walk past your booth. Close to the entrance is nice, as is close to the refreshment stand. Do research on past years' shows to see what potential results you can expect and what supplies you will be expected to have. Keep at least five people involved at all times, so you have enough prospectors to handle the prospects. Bring in the business builders from your downline to do this–and so they can learn in the process, and develop a strong loyalty to you and the team you're building.

People rarely wait around at expos until you get a chance to talk to them. They look quickly and move on to the rest of the show unless you or your people give them a reason to stay and talk. You and your business builders have to give them a reason to do so.

Have good phone veterans ready to make the calls immediately, before the leads are old and cold. It costs you money to get leads. Blowing a lead is *not* what you want to let happen! That's *not* why you went to the expo and got the lead in the first place! This follow-up step is as important as a follow-through in a golf swing. Make sure the right people call the prospects–right away! Make those calls that night or the next day. Don't give the prospect time to forget you.

Another popular form of prospecting is cold calling. This is a very hard approach, suggested only for thick-skinned networkers who can handle massive rejection. Cold-calling should only be used after every referral and every contact you have has been reached.

Let's talk about who you should be calling to cold call effectively. I recommend using this method with only the following types of people:

The first person I would cold call is a sales and marketing professional, stock broker, Realtor, insurance agent, owner of a marketing company or car salesman. They understand marketing, know what you're doing, and are probably less likely to hang up on a fellow professional. They're pre-qualified by being in professions dedicated to making money in sales.

The second type of people that I would cold call are those already involved with residual income businesses–cell phone company salespeople, and network marketers working in another program, for example. This can be really profitable, but is incredibly challenging. Try calling inventors–they understand the power of earning money for a long period of time based on a one-time effort. Also, telemarketers can be good prospects. They're always looking for an easier way to make more money, and rejection doesn't bother them–they cold-call for a living!

Don't waste your energy calling out of the white pages. Grab the Yellow Pages, look under these professions, and cold-call them.

Make a *lead notebook*. A lead notebook is a list of every name and phone number of every person you cold call. Write notes on each person, for every call you make to them, for when you make follow up calls in the future if they don't give you the appointment right away. Use the key points you have written down on this page to start building a relationship so they are no longer cold prospects when you make the second or later follow-up call.

When I did a lot of cold calling, I used the following script:

"Hi, is Jerry in the office? Hi, Jerry. We don't know each other yet, but I know you're a great insurance agent. You and I have something in common. Both our businesses work on referral sales. In the business I'm associated with, I've seen a lot of insurance agents generate an extra $5,000 a month or more–part-time! This opportunity creates residual income. They didn't jeopardize their primary business at all. Actually, they enhanced it with new referrals. I would be honored, at your convenience, to treat you to lunch near your office. I can show you what my business entails with a short visual presentation. At the very least, I have a few referrals to offer you, people who need a good insurance plan. I like to do business with people who do business with me. Is 12 noon, Tuesday or Thursday, a good time for us to meet at the diner right across the street from your office?"

This cold call technique (1) creates curiosity, (2) compliments the person, (3) offers a free lunch, (4) offers referrals, (5) shows the person that others in his or her profession have become successful in this, and (6) appeals to a need for extra residual income the person might be looking for. Because of your lack of rapport with the person on the other end of the phone, the odds of getting an appointment on the first call are 1 or 2 out of 10, if you are good. However, good follow-up, using this technique with your lead notebook, will generate more appointments down the road.

Cold calling is similar to all prospecting techniques in that it is a numbers game. The more calls or contacts you make, the more appointments and potential sign-ups you will have. In cold calling, before you get on the phone you must expect prospects to behave disrespectfully. You will be hung up on, yelled at, or even threatened. (Ask any telemarketer.) *Don't take it personally!* The people you call are frustrated with you out of a lack of information. You have to view it as their loss. Remember, you're offering a *pot of gold* to people. Practice makes perfect in finding the best way to make them understand that. Realize that if it takes you a thousand cold calls to get one great person, it was well worth your effort.

Thomas Edison needed 9,999 attempts before he harnessed electricity to create the first electric light bulb. We're all very glad–every day!–that he was persistent and had a "keep trying until you get it right; practice makes perfect" attitude. (Remember the last time you tried to live with candles during a power outage?)

108

Prospecting can and should be done at reunions, social functions and family occasions. These are perfect avenues for talking to people whom you might or might not know well who you don't see often, but with whom you have something in common. Take advantage of these occasions by getting phone numbers. *Don't try to pitch the opportunity, that night, to anyone.* Get each person's phone number and promise to call at a mutually agreeable time.

I have a five-foot rule that goes like this: If someone sharp is within five feet of me, I want to approach and prospect him or her. Act positively. Dress professionally. Most of all, create curiosity and be a good listener. Look for sharp people who live in your local area.

Here's a good way to subtly get into a conversation about your business:

"Hey, Bob, long time no see. What are you doing these days?" When he asks you what you are doing, let him know that you're working part-time at starting your own business with a marketing company that's doing very well–and you're doing very well with it. Let him know that you feel it's fate that the two of you are meeting again, because you believe he can do great things in this new business. Tell him you're looking for partners. On face-to-face interactions, your goal is to get phone numbers and remind each prospect that you will be calling in the next forty-eight hours for an appointment.

You can also prospect using direct mail, radio, infomercials, and other mass media techniques. Unless you have past experience doing this, and a big up-front amount to spend to get the marketing started, I would not recommend these techniques of prospecting. They are for when you've created a major organization, have become a top producer for your company, and are bringing in big money each month. When you reach the earning level that gives you that kind of money, you can afford to spend some of it to make still more money.

Here's a quick summary of the *do's* in the art of prospecting:

Create curiosity.
Contact as many people as possible.
Recruit people at your business level and higher.
Do what feels comfortable to you and works for you.
Do what is cost-effective.
Remember the five-foot rule.
Act professionally.
Follow up with people who don't give you an appointment.
Get referrals.
Work your warm list and lukewarm list first.
Remember that you're doing a favor for the person you're prospecting.
Some will, some won't, so what? Go on to the next name.

Remember this formula:

Prospecting equals appointments, equals sign-ups, equals increase in residual income and increase in status.

The Art of Inviting a Prospect to Join

Inviting takes many forms but commonly involves you, either in person or on the phone, attempting to set an appointment with one of your prospects who is not yet involved in your business.

The formula–prospects equals appointments equals sign-ups equals increased income and status–illustrates the point that the more prospecting calls you make and the more in-person meetings you have, the more appointments you will have, and the higher your income will become.

Thus, your ability to sow the seeds of your income garden, so to speak, results from prospecting. The more seeds you plant, the more crops you will harvest–just like a farmer will harvest more crops if he plants the right number of seeds per acre, plants more acres, and tends his plants well.

However, it is not the number of calls you make; it's the percentage of the people you call whom you *actually meet* that's the key to current and residual income. *That's a controllable factor.* I'll show you how to prospect effectively so that you will see at least a 50% phone-call to appointment ratio. After you read this chapter you should be able to get appointments from one out of two prospecting calls from your warm or lukewarm list.

Before I give you scripts to use for prospecting these people and how to invite them, it's critical to understand certain things before you pick up the phone and make your first call.

It is not the words you say. It is the music that you play.

A successful prospector won't just *read* these scripts (like some first-grader reading *See Jack Run*) but will do it with *enthusiasm, excitement and urgency.* Whether you are a quiet person or a naturally extroverted loudmouth, you need to raise the excitement of your voice level one notch (or more) to make the person you are prospecting take immediate note that you're serious about what you are doing. Take each of these scripts and change any wording necessary to *make it your own.* Your scripts should be comfortable for you to read. If they are not, you'll sound like you're reading someone else's words, and listeners hear that *instantly.* Good scripts allow for whatever variations may seem appropriate for use with each prospect.

Some will meet you; some won't meet you; some won't do it right now. Get referrals from them and prospect again.

Remember that prospecting is a numbers game. It is not a gamble like the lottery or blackjack because the more prospecting you do, the better your odds get.

Your prospecting skills won't become fair until you prospect badly.

Your prospecting won't become good until you've done it fair-to-middling. While prospecting badly won't bring many people into your organization, it will bring in *some.* (Yes, you *do* have to start *somewhere!*) People who never get better than fair-to-middling have built quite respectable organizations and incomes.

You won't be a *great* prospector until you become a fair-to-middling prospector, and progress to become a good prospector.

While perhaps only a few people qualify as "great" prospectors, if you care to be hard-nosed about the definition, fair-to-middling and good prospecting produces surprisingly good results.

Practice *does indeed* make perfect. The more you prospect, the better you'll get at it and the better your results will be. "Great," as I've used the word above, doesn't really matter. Yes, it's nice if everyone in your upline and downline thinks you're a great prospector, but all that matters is that you keep prospecting and keep working to do it better next time. All that matters is "better" by your personal standards. Like runners who are not world-class milers or marathoners, apply their term, *personal best* to your prospecting. Their personal best is the best time they, personally, have done for whatever distance they run. Your personal best is the current best you've done in prospecting. Always strive to do and to improve your personal best.

Be in a good mood before you get on the phone. If you've had a rushed, tense, day, take time to relax, calm down, and center your focus on what you're about to do.

Please note: ninety percent of your invitation success is determined not by *what you say* but by *how you say it.*

Don't get emotional. Everyone has friends or family members who say, "Are you *crazy*? I can't believe you're into *that!* No, I don't want to look at your new business!"

Realize that if you stay focused and continue to prospect past these *dream stealers*, who love you so much they're scared of change for you, some day you'll prove to them that you're the smart one. When I made $225,000 in one month in my 48th month in the business I'm currently with, I sent a note to every friend and family member who thought my business would fail. I invited them all to a nationwide satellite TV program where they could watch me accept my check and see and hear all the applause that followed. That was the end of any negativity I ever received. If you stay focused on how important prospecting is, you will keep

112

planting those seeds through the up and down times of your networking business.

I recommend that you stay on the phone for at least an hour whenever you schedule a cold-calling session. You will get into a routine, and achieve a comfort level, that will let you set a higher percentage of appointments the longer you stay on the phone. This is a better strategy than making a call here and a call there during the week.

I usually make calls between 7 PM and 10 PM, Sunday night through Thursday night. People are more likely to be home during evening hours. Before seven, they may be eating dinner. After ten they may be in bed. Work is not the preferable environment in which to invite someone, but if that's the only time you can call, then call during working hours. Just be aware you're more likely to encounter rejection.

I'll give you several generic scripts with which to invite your warm and lukewarm prospects. The first part of every "how to invite" script is called FORM. This stands for Family, Occupation, Recreation and Money.

The reason you use these scripts is simple. You don't want someone to think the only reason you are calling them is to recruit them. FORM breaks the ice and allows you to draw your prospect into a conversation about his or her needs, desires, concerns, and worries, just as you might in everyday conversation. This opening technique gives you the opportunity to identify a hot button. A hot button is a pain the person you're calling suffers.

For instance, suppose the person you're calling says, "Marian and I are working a lot of overtime and not spending quality time together or with our children anymore because we are starting a college tuition fund for Max," or, "I don't enjoy my job. I look at the clock thirty times a day, just waiting for it to be 5 PM, but I need the money so I do it over and over again, every single day."

These people are crying out for the opportunity you offer. These statements and others like them are the hot buttons which you should use to open up the invitation. These hot buttons identify the needs and problems of this particular person. When you identify

113

the hot button, press it (carefully, tactfully) to show him or her that you can offer an opportunity to do something about those needs and problems. When the person responds, you're well on the way to a sign-up. Once you go through the small talk, here are some scripts to use. Decide which one is best for each individual you are calling. Your choice of script, and your personal variations on it, will depend on the person.

Script 1: The "I'm in a New Business" Opener

Use this approach when you meet someone at a party, at church, a wedding, or any occasion when you encounter a person who might be a prospect, but you don't have or want to take time for a full presentation. Remember, you want to set up an appointment at a time and in a setting which allows the person focus on your opportunity without distractions.

At some point, your prospect will ask what's new and exciting with you.

You answer, "I've started a new business. I'm an executive with a marketing company which markets environmentally safe products. It's fabulous. I'd love to tell you all about it some time, but right now I have to run. Why don't I call you and we'll get together? What's your number?"

Script 2: The "Starting a Home-based Business" Opener

"I help people start their own home-based businesses with no risk."

Script 3: The "Home-based Business" Hot Button

"If you had a job with no boss and no overhead expenses and could work your own hours at home with an excellent income, would you be interested?"

Script 4: The "Products Work And Save You Money" Opener

"Are you into products that work and save you money?"

Script 5: The "Are You With?" Opener

"Are you with (name of company)?"

Script 6: The "Right Thing" Opener

"If the right thing came along, and I mean it was really the right opportunity, would you have an interest in increasing your income?"

Let the prospect respond.

"It's an American company called _____ . I'm not saying it would be for you, but you need to take a look at it and judge it for yourself."

Script 7: The "How Are We Going to Pay For–?" Opener

"Do you have twenty minutes to hear how we are going to pay our college tuition, retirement, and buy a new car? Great. I'd love to set up an appointment with you, either Tuesday or Thursday at noon."

Script 8: The "Strapped for Cash, Need a Second Income" Hot Button

"You know, we were the same way. I was thinking about getting a second job to help our budget, but then we started a little home-based business. I know lots of people who have developed a second income in a very short time. Ours is already growing. It's really simpler than getting another job. No commuting, daycare and such, and I get to stay home. If you like, I'll come over and share with you what I'm doing. We can watch a video that explains the whole concept."

115

Script 9: The "Everything's Too Expensive" Hot Button

"I know how you feel. We recently joined a great consumer discount company that is helping. They offer savings on every household product, and on long distance telephone services. If you're interested in saving money, too, I could show you our catalog."

Script 10: The "Health-conscious" Hot Button

"Hey, we found some fabulous natural, nontoxic products we can buy wholesale, direct from the factory. They're more effective, completely safe for our family, and save us money every month. Are you interested?"

Script 11: the "Weight-conscious" Hot Button

"Boy, we found a terrific program for wellness and weight control that is on the cutting edge of technology. We really need to sit down and talk about this. When can we get together?"

Script 12: The "Stay at Home Mom" Hot Button

"You know, it's getting tougher and tougher to make it on one income, but we want one of us to be able to stay home with the kids. We recently started a business that lets us work at home to earn a second income. Want to hear about it sometime?"

Script 13: The "Cold Contact Service Person or Waiter/Waitress" Approach

"You know, you've provided us excellent service. Can I ask you a question? Are you getting paid what you're worth here? I have a business I think you'd love and excel in. It's the best part-time business I ever heard of. It will pay you what you are worth. Can we meet for coffee and I'll give you some of the details?"

116

Script 14: The "MLM Frustratees" Hot Button

"You know, I'm like you. I was in one of those companies. I didn't make any money. In fact, I lost money. But I finally found a company that has their act together. They got rid of all the negatives and red flags that bugged me about those other guys. Let's get together and I'll show you how it's different from anything you've ever looked at. I know you've already tried company X, but if I showed you how to do it differently, you'd make money. Want to hear about it?"

Script 15: The "Out of Town Prospect" Approach

Send the prospect a copy of the video and the enrollment forms. Throw in a bag of microwave popcorn (everyone likes an unexpected treat). "I've started a business with a company called ____. I'd really like you to take a look at it. I'll send you a video with information about our company. I'll call you back in a few days. If you have any questions, write them down and I'll answer them when I call you."

Script 16: The "Credibility" Approach

"Do I have credibility with you?" (Wait for their answer) "Then would you give me the courtesy of thirty minutes to sit down with you and tell you about a company I'm excited about?"

Script 17: The "Work Together" Approach

"I've discovered a company called ____. I think we can make some money if we work together on it. What do you say?"

117

Script 18: The "Business Owner" Approach

"You must work a lot of hours, don't you? You work hard for your money, don't you? I need to talk to you about a business where my customers buy every month with no additional effort on my part. When can we set up a meeting?"

Script 19: The "Meeting Invitation" Approach

"Say, John, I'm checking out a new business called _____. I'm going to a business presentation on Thursday and wonder if you'd like to go with me and give me your opinion. Great! I'll pick you up at your place at 6 PM."

Script 20: The "If I Could Show You...Would You Give Me 15 to 30 Minutes of Your Time?" Approach

There are a lot of variations on this script. It adapts easily to whatever you determine is the hot button to which a person will respond. Some examples:

"If I could show you a way to earn your car payment without risk, would you give me 15 to 30 minutes?"

"If I could show you a way to earn your mortgage payment without risk, would you give me 30 minutes?

"If I could show you a way to help you create retirement income without risk, would you give me 30 minutes?"

"If I could show you a way to make a lot of money without risk, would you give me 30 minutes of your time?"

"If I could show you something that made total sense and you didn't have to sell anything, you didn't have to invest anything, and you could make an extra $_____ this year, would you give me 30 minutes of your time?"

Some of the major objectives of the actual approach to any prospect are:

(1) To compliment

118

(2) To create curiosity

(3) To control the conversation

(4) To get absolute commitment for the date and time when they're going to meet you.

Some helpful tips

Don't overexpose it.

Keep it short and simple. (KISS theory; sometimes also translated as, Keep it simple, stupid.) I prefer my version, Keep it Simple and Smooth, because it's not negative.

Make notes before you call.

If it is worth doing, it's worth doing right.

Always have a script in front of you.

Arouse curiosity.

Be excited–it's the music, not the words.

Never hesitate after the approach.

Get a commitment. "Is Monday or Wednesday at 8 p.m. better for you?"

Always carry a calendar with you, and your contact list.

Ask questions. The person who asks questions controls the conversation.

Never give into their curiosity.

Show the opportunity to the husband and wife together, unless it's impossible.

Get firm commitments. When you confirm, say, "Did I tell you 7 or 7:30?

Please don't be early, please don't be late.

Practice, practice, practice makes *permanent*, not perfect.

Do it now and do it often.

Don't tell anything until you can tell it all.

No more 15-minute phone presentations.

Follow the four Cs: Compliment, Create Curiosity, Control the Conversation, and Get Their Commitment.

Take it seriously. You could have a *huge* business with immense potential to create and maintain your wealth.

Always have a back-up night if a prospect can't meet when you suggest, or calls and cancels for any reason–especially if the reason is legitimate. If the reason the person wants to cancel is clearly a weasel-out-of-it response, have alternative nights ready to offer. If the person finds reasons not to meet at any time, even on a night of his or her own choosing, then you're probably being told that this individual was a lousy prospect in the first place–and you don't want to waste time on non-prospects.

It's important that you've made plans to share your business–your "pot of gold" gift–with each prospect. Go out, meet, present, and follow the famous Nike slogan: *Just do it!*

Team up. Calendaring and partnering are essential to your success. Go upline.

Communication with your upline, on a daily basis, is crucial.

Get 3-way calling.

Use the strapped for cash approach. "You know, we were the same way. I was even thinking about getting a second job to help our budget. But when we started a little home-based business called _____, I met lots of people who have developed a significant second income in a very short time."

Use the Feel, Felt, Found method. "Hey, I know exactly how you feel. I felt the same way. Then I found a company called ___ __ and discovered that this system really works. Let's get together and talk about it."

Some criteria I look for in prospecting are:

Look for people who are honest, ambitious, happy, successful at something, have home-based business experience, have respectability, credibility, dress upscale, are likeable, walk as if there is a cape flowing behind them, and are aggressive and assertive (without being obnoxious about it).

Let people qualify themselves.

CHAPTER SIX

PRESENTATIONS: FIFTY PERCENT SHOW BIZ– *ONE HUNDRED PERCENT SINCERITY!*

Making effective presentations to prospects is one of the most important keys to helping your organization grow. This chapter will cover different presentation formats you can use, the six steps to perfecting your presentation *and the critical closing techniques at the end of your presentation.*
The four major presentation formats are:

1. Telephone presentations
2. Two-on-ones
3. In-home or small group meetings.
4. At a hotel.

The first popular presentation method is by telephone. Whether you are presenting to one or one thousand people, a telephone presentation can be done in your shorts sitting in your kitchen. To set up a presentation using this format for one or two people, all you need is three-way calling. This allows you to connect two people with you. When using this method, have your presentation book in front of you and picture yourself right in front of the prospects, i.e., do the same presentation as if the people were in front of you, but without the visual aides you would use face-to-face. At the end of the presentation, fax or FedEx sign-up forms to your new people. Create urgency.

Another telephone approach is to have someone in your organization invite a group of potential new enrollees to come to his or her home. At the pre-arranged time, when you know the group has gathered, you call the person who has set up the meeting and is hosting the presentation. Your meeting host has a speakerphone set up in the middle of the group.

Give the presentation as you would give it if the prospects were right in front of you. Although you are not physically in the room with the prospects, you can use visual aids. You have told the host to photocopy key pages of your presentation and put them in front of each new person to read along with you as you make your presentation, explaining the business. The younger your audience–that is, the more they've grown up on television and are visually-oriented–the more important is it to have something visual to show them. The old "a picture is worth a thousand words" line, today, should perhaps become, "if they can't see it, they can't understand it."

At the end of your presentation, the host passes out sign-up forms and enrolls the new customers. Walk through the paperwork over the speakerphone, if possible. The host can answer any questions that are more easily answered on the spot instead of over the phone.

If some of your guests don't sign up at the meeting–you won't get them all–do three-way calls to them, with the host, within the first forty-eight hours after the initial phone presentation. Use your credibility to encourage the guests to enroll. Your credibility is important in helping the host answer the concerns and questions, and alleviating the skepticism these more hesitant guests probably have. If they didn't have questions and feel skeptical, they'd likely have signed up at the meeting, so assume you'll be dealing with real concerns when you call these people back.

This follow-through is like a golf swing. If you don't follow through in golf, your game suffers enormously. The same is true in closing the host's guests. If you don't follow through, you'll lose many potential enrollees. The follow-through gives you a second chance to bring them on board.

Your follow-through creates two things. First, it gets the people who didn't join the night of your phone presentation to sign up. Second, it shows the host that you're committed to teaming up and helping him or her build the business. Your commitment will give the host confidence that it will pay to have more of these meetings. That confidence will duplicate itself once the host is ready to have other people in his or her organization set up these conference calls, and he or she is ready to take over your role in making the presentation and doing the follow-up. This is how you multiply yourself for ever-greater profits.

You can also do telephone presentations using a conference call provider. These providers are in business to facilitate conference calls for large and small businesses–and for people like you. At your request, they reserve a certain number of lines for your conference call. You can book lines for a conference call to five, twenty, one hundred, or even thousands of people, and give your presentation to as many people as you can get on the call.

The conference call can be made using a toll-free number for the participants, or a toll number where each participant pays for the long-distance charges. The toll-free call costs you a lot more, but it will get more response from new prospects. Members of your organization should be willing to pay for the knowledge you impart on such a call. This technique is an excellent way of training your organization and helping your business grow outside the area in which you live.

The advantages of a phone presentation are:

1. You are signing up people all over the country, and even all over the world, all at once.
2. It is cost effective. There are no airline or hotel expenses.
3. It is time efficient. In one hour, you can potentially close many new customers.
4. It helps people in your organization get off to a good start.

5. It allows you to invite a guest speaker from out of your area to speak on the call.
6. You can tape your presentation and use the same one over and over again, once you get a speech that maximizes the results you want.

However, there are some disadvantages.

The first disadvantage is that there is no personal contact. Your sincerity is not as obvious as if you were present, and your closing techniques and sign-up procedure will not run as smoothly as if you were there to present and supervise it in person.

Second, the percentage of people who sign up will be lower than if you had used the direct-contact approach.

Third, more follow-up will be needed to sign up the people from the initial presentation.

Fourth, you will generate less excitement. That usually means that your new people will do less work to start their business quickly.

Fifth and last, there is more attrition of people with this approach because of the lack of person-to-person contact.

I recommend this approach only if you are expanding an organization into an area more than a hundred miles from your home, or you have many hundreds of people in your organization who can plug into your system, but are too far away to see you give your presentation in person.

As computer video-conferencing becomes more common and is something anyone with a computer can arrange, some of the disadvantages will be mitigated. How much more effective you can be on a video conference call remains to be seen. The answer to that one will have to wait for technology to catch up. But, if you and your host are into computers, or perhaps use video conferencing in your businesses, and can arrange a video conference, give it a try and see what happens. You could find yourself on the cutting edge of marketing! (But you can't do a video-conference call sitting at the kitchen table in your shorts!)

124

The second type of presentation is a two-on-one. In a two-on-one, you do a meeting for one person, partnering with and supporting/training someone new in your organization to give the presentation. If John is new in your business and you and John go to his Aunt Sally's house to make a presentation to her, that's a two-on-one.

Two-on-ones, if at all possible, should be done at the prospect's home or office. If you invite one guest to your home, the chance of a no-show or cancellation is much higher than if you go to the prospect's house. When a two-on-one is done at the prospect's home or office, the person will almost certainly have a method of payment–normally a credit card–ready to sign up. If the spouse is also present, that's always a plus.

In building my business in this industry, the majority of my success has been through two-on-one presentations. The technique has a number of benefits.

1. It is incredibly duplicatable. Duplication is the key to growth within your organization. Not everyone will feel capable or comfortable in front of a large group.

2. You can tailor your presentation to the person you are presenting to. If you are presenting to a 75-year-old grandmother who made $10,000 a year in the best years of her working life, and your next prospect is a 42-year-old insurance agent routinely earning six figures, a two-on-one gives you flexibility to identify and cover the points critical to each prospect's needs and interests.

3. Your sign-up percentage is highest with this approach.

4. Questions, concerns and skepticism can be most easily dealt with in a two-on-one. You can isolate an objection and give it all the time and detail needed to overcome it. In a group or phone presentation, you have to give a general answer and move on.

5. Because you are presenting to one person, the person feels more pressure to make a decision right away. Less follow-up is required.

125

6.   A two-on-one creates the most excitement possible because the new person leaves with a clear understanding of the business, benefits and the income potential. Excitement = action. Action = many appointments. Many appointments = many new customers in your business.

Another popular way of presenting is in the small group setting, also called an in-home presentation. This is where someone new in your organization invites some of his or her friends, family or colleagues to come to their home to hear your presentation. The size of the group is limited by the size of the host's home. (This is also true of the group presentation by phone.)

If you are going to do a group meeting in person, make sure the host of this presentation has prepared for it properly. First, he or she must confirm all guests the night before. Invite twice as many prospects as you would like to show up, since fifty percent of your confirmed guests will be no-shows.

Make the time and place clear, and provide good directions. Do your presentation around a table, not in a standing-up format, so the presenter can be at the same level as the guests. Serve some non-alcoholic beverages, but no meals or alcohol, before or during the meeting.

Make sure the host does a good job introducing the opportunity, and introducing you, before you begin your presentation. The host's pre-presentation remarks are crucial in assuring the attentiveness of the guests while you are doing presenting.

If children or pets are present, make sure they don't interfere with the presentation while it is in progress. Have a complete product or service display in the room at the start of the presentation and while the presentation is being given.

Start the presentation no later than ten minutes after the scheduled time. It is not right to penalize people who are interested and arrived on time.

Compliment the host during your presentation. Obviously, that earns you points with the guests and makes it easier when you get to the close. Make sure the host has all the sign-up forms and other materials ready for the close.

If possible, invite the same type of people to a presentation, i.e., don't mix old blue collar friends with young, successful white collar relatives.

A group meeting can be a powerful way to enroll a lot of new customers and potential business builders if these guidelines are followed. Excitement is really high when you have a dining room full of people all signing up because everyone has seen that it's a really good business. You also can get more time commitment to the business from your host if he or she sees it working and feels the excitement that's been generated.

There is a risk, though, that one negative person in the group could kill everyone's interest. This has happened to me on many occasions. Try to avoid this by discouraging a prospect who sounds negative when responding to your phone call. If a person sounds negative, do your presentation to that prospect two-on-one.

If someone becomes negative during the presentation, tell them that all questions and concerns will be answered at the end of the presentation. That allows a steady flow of information during your talk. If possible, get the host to take that guest into another room so his or her negativity won't rub off on anyone else.

A group meeting is effective if the presenter is a seasoned veteran and the host lays out the preliminaries well. I recommend that you use group meetings for family and friends whom you feel will benefit from becoming customers, and use on two-on-ones for potential business builders. Pre-judging prospects is not a perfect science, so don't be surprised if you learn during a presentation that someone isn't what you expected. Learn to be flexible in the way you deal with groups and individual prospects.

A hotel meeting is the last major presentation method.

For this type of presentation, a seasoned veteran with a lot of experience chooses a city where there's a large concentration of business builders. He or she does a presentation to anywhere from 20 and 2,000 people in a hotel meeting room.

The meeting is usually set up theater-style. When planning a meeting of this size and type, follow these guidelines:

1. Give ample notice about the meeting via mail, phone or e-mail (or all three) to all marketers in the area. You want them to actively promote the meeting so attendance will be at the highest possible level.

2. Set up the meeting with fewer chairs than the number of people you expect to have. More chairs can be set up as people arrive. This "overflow crowd" image creates excitement. There's nothing worse than a bunch of empty seats! Empty seats make it look as if you didn't get the turnout you expected! Hotels can accommodate this, if you tell them to be ready for more people. (You won't be the first to use this technique at any well-run hotel!)

3. Make sure that all guests are seated next to their hosts and that you sit with your people. That assures that when the sign-up process begins you will be near your people and their guests.

4. Have a sign-in sheet for all guests, with spaces for each person's address and phone number, and who invited them. Use a separate sign-in sheet for your people who are already in the business. The guest sheet can be used as a follow-up to get those who attended enrolled in the future. The other sheet can be used to call all marketing executives to promote future meetings.

5. Have a great product/service display in the front of the room. Make sure all the lighting, microphones, overhead projectors, screens, and other equipment needed for the meeting are set up and working before people arrive. Check and double check, not only to assure that everything is working, but that the people who will operate the equipment know how to do so.

6. Make sure all the top people within your organization have name tags and are greeting all guests as they enter.

7.   Be very friendly. Take time at the beginning of your meeting to recognize your people and acknowledge everyone's accomplishments. This is one of the biggest reasons why people go to meetings and work for your business. It also builds the credibility of your people in the eyes of their guests.

8.   Make sure there is ample water, the room temperature is comfortable, and everyone has a pad and pen to take notes with.

9.   Have a powerful close. Many great presenters do a wonderful presentation but don't close the guests in the audience. I recommend that the presenter walk the audience through the sign-up form, step-by-step, using an overhead projector so everyone can see what line is being talked about, i.e., have a sample sign-up form on a transparency. This way some people who otherwise might not sign up will become new customers immediately–right there, that night. You might not close them otherwise, perhaps not even with the best follow-up. This closing technique creates more customers for you and your organization. When your people see their invited guests signing up, it makes them excited about bringing more guests to future meetings.

10.   Keep all receipts for these meetings. They represent a 50% tax write-off for you–and that's not small change, even if you only do one meeting a year on this scale. Certain costs of other meetings are deductible, too. Check with your accountant or tax advisor.

11.   Try to select the same hotel for all of your functions and have them all on the same day of the week. This will allow you to negotiate a lower rate for your meeting room at the hotel and also let your customers get used to a certain schedule. They won't have to dig out their maps. For example, a 7:00 PM presentation the first Monday of the month and a 10:00 AM training the third Sunday of the

month, at your chosen hotel, is the kind of consistency that
will pay off.

12. Make sure your presentation takes the amount of time you
advertised it to be. If you said the meeting would be from
7:00 PM to 9:00 PM, start by 7:10 and end by 9:10, *no
later!* A hotel meeting is a good forum for a training
session. It may be equally good for a once a month
business briefing, with a guest speaker whenever possible

Now that you know and understand the four popular
presentation methods and the pros and cons and the dos and don'ts
of each, you should also understand the importance of giving the
best presentation you can. There are six steps to giving a perfect
presentation, each with its set of sub-steps.

The first step in giving a presentation to a new prospect is
to have a professional presentation manual or booklet to leaf
through, showing the prospect something visual as you talk.

Remember, a picture is worth a thousand words.

This will build your credibility (and that of the company you
represent), and save you from having to memorize what you want
to say. Most of all, a booklet or manual is duplicatable for others
to use in your organization down the road—and your prospect can
see that he or she will have the same materials to help build his or
her business.

One you have put together good, solid material, you need to
work on your attitude. Having a positive attitude in the way you
say things in your presentation is more important than being a
great speaker. It is often not what you say but how positively you
say it that will determine your results. You are selling *yourself*
more than you are selling the company or the opportunity you
represent—especially in the first part of the presentation. Sell
yourself first. *Then* you become credible and can sell the
opportunity.

The last item you need to consider prior to presenting is how
your dress—the appearance you present to prospects. I believe in
matching, or cloning. That means you should dress slightly better

than the prospects to whom you are going to present the opportunity. You don't want to look like an overdressed insurance salesman when presenting to a couple in shorts in a trailer park. Similarly, you also don't want to wear casual attire, say jeans and a tee-shirt, when presenting to someone during their lunch break in a corporate environment.

After your materials, posture and dress are finalized, you are ready to make presentations. Remember this formula in network marketing: phone calls = appointments; appointments = presentations; presentations = new sign-ups; new sign-ups = increased income and status.

The presentation is the heart of the whole equation for how successful you will be and how quickly success will come.

It is absolutely true that you have to do several bad presentations before you make an okay presentation and you have to do several okay presentations before you make a good presentation and you have to do a good presentation before you do a great presentation. Practice makes perfect.

Because you are selling *yourself first*, the obvious first step in a perfect presentation is your story.

Your story should be three to five minutes long. This time allows you to relate to the prospect on a personal level before you become a salesperson presenting an opportunity. It also might hit on a common need or desire you and your prospects share, which could create a bond between the two of you.

Your story should include your *why*.

Why did you choose the business that you are presenting over everything else out there? List some advantages you saw when looking at your business.

The second thing your story should include is your family background. Talk about your career and family life and how this business fits in.

The third thing your story should include is a description of your needs and goals for your business. Paint a dream-building picture of your personal motivations which led you to work with the company you represent. Give the prospect a realistic, honest and exciting account of your financial goals for the next one, three and five years with your business.

Fourth, talk briefly about any skepticism or reservations you had when you first looked at this opportunity. Use the Feel, Felt, Found approach to remove any questions or challenges your prospects might have. For example, "I feel this is a great opportunity, although I felt skeptical when I first saw the presentation. But once I did my research on the company and what it offered me, I found there were no holes in it at all."

At the end of your story, reiterate the benefits you saw in the business. Talk about how much progress you've already made. If there are stories from people in your upline, use them! Tell the prospect(s) what you will cover and how long the presentation will be.

Here's an example of a story you can model yours after.

"Hi, my name is (your name). I'm going to tell you about a part-time business I'm doing that I'm really excited about. The benefits I saw when I was shown this opportunity were that it has no risk, provides great training and support, and part-time people like me can make an extra one or two thousand dollars a month within six to twelve months. I've met many who are already there. I live in Boynton Beach, Florida and have been a financial analyst for AT&T since I graduated from college four years ago. I saw that, financially I was able to pay the bills but could not save or get ahead. I believe in the saying that if you continue to do what you have always done to make money, you will get the same results in the future, but if you add something to your full-time job for a couple of years, you could reach your dreams. I wasn't reaching my dreams in the corporate world, and didn't want to risk either my money or my profession. I saw this business as my avenue to reach my dreams and aspirations. In my first month with the company, I made $320. I will be earning $3,000 a month, part time, by the end of the year. In the next two years, this company will help me put a down payment on a home and pay off my credit card debt. When I first saw the presentation, I was skeptical because I had heard of people losing money in these types of businesses, but I was smart enough to test drive this opportunity. I learned that there was nothing else like it out there. This, I believe, is a unique opportunity."

This part of the presentation is like the drive off the tee in golf, which sets up the rest of the hole. Your story should be honest, sincere, straight from the heart and let you bond with, excite, and knock skepticism out of the prospect.

The second part of a perfect presentation is the company's story.

Once you have told your prospect about yourself, take five minutes or so to talk about the company you are representing. This is where your presentation should be visual. Use your manual or booklet. A prospect wants to hear enough to make him or her feel that the business will last for a lifetime, but going over too much background information will turn off and bore a prospect.

I recommend covering the following facts about a company:

1. How old is the company, and where is it located?
2. What does the company market, and through what distribution network?
3. Talk about the company's financial statistics with Dun & Bradstreet, if possible.
4. Who are the owners? What is the background experience of the corporate management?
5. What were the company's sales last year? What are their realistic goals for this year?
6. Any awards, magazine articles or other outside recognition that give credibility to the company should be mentioned.

In this portion of the presentation it's important to make sure the prospect will leave with a clear, concise, and positive feeling that the business you are representing will last forever and is a very solid operation. A big credibility factor for you in this part of the presentation is whether you have visited the company headquarters, met the president, and/or attended a company convention. Then you will be able to talk about your own, direct, personal experience.

The heart of the presentation is the third part, in which you present the products and/or services your company is selling. Keep in mind that most people who listen to your presentation will never do the business as aggressively as you, but all of them have the potential to become *lifetime customers* if they understand the benefits of becoming a customer.

Some phrases you can use in presenting the products and services are:

"If I never made another nickel in this business, I still would be using the products and services every month, because of their low cost, high quality and convenience."

"The products and services are the backbone of the entire opportunity. They are responsible for every dime of income is paid to us. If our products and services were not exceptional in quality and reasonably priced, our reorder rate would not be _____ percent." Give frequent comparisons between the products and services you are marketing versus the competition.

The three main sizzle points that generate interest are price, quality and convenience. These are the three things people want in something they purchase.

Talk about price. Use graphs, illustrations or charts showing the cost per use of your product or service compared to competitors. Every potential customer wants a good deal. If you can show them the cost savings, it will help in convincing your prospects to try your company's items.

After the price, shoppers want to be educated about the quality advantages of your products. Remember, people's first inclination is that they don't like change, and change is exactly what you're attempting to convince them to do. If any major reputable agency has performed quality tests on your products, mention these findings. If the company is a member of PITA, your products are FDA registered, are environmentally safe, have patents, exclusivity, or are manufactured in the company's plants, are written up in medical journals, or are unique in any way compared to the competition, these points need to be made.

However, you don't want to get into complex details of ingredients or processing techniques in an initial presentation. This could diminish your prospect's interest level. The rule of thumb, remember, is, *keep it simple and smooth–KISS.*

When talking about the quality of what you're selling, use personal testimonies about what products you like and why. Stories sell. Stories help you describe in an honest and simple way what the products and services could offer your prospect. For example, you could give the example of the company's shave gel–no irritation or burning. If a shave gel is not among their products, find a product to talk about that your listener will relate to.

The last point you should mention is the refund policy. If your company has a 100% trial period during which a new customer can try the products, risk-free, with no obligation, that's a big selling point. You're helping the new person establish a comfort level with the products and the company, so he or she will want to give your company's items a try.

Convenience can also be a major factor in new person's decision to join. In today's families, it is highly likely that both the husband and wife work. Especially for two-income families, saving time shopping is highly advantageous. If your company's products can be delivered to your potential prospect's home quickly, in less than five business days, be sure to mention this benefit in your presentation. Rapid delivery is a major benefit for most families.

The fourth step in your presentation is an explanation of the compensation plan. This is where you can excite the new prospect with the enticing potential of earning extra residual income. No matter what your compensation plan entails, you must first explain what residual income is. It's not a familiar term for most people.

This is how to explain it: "Residual income is income that comes in month after month, year after year, possibly for your entire lifetime, because of an action you took once. You sign up a new customer by doing a one-time presentation about the business.

Each month, for years and years thereafter, as long as that person remains a customer, our company will pay you a bonus on every order for goods and services placed by that customer, even if you never talk to that customer again. Do you see the advantage this has over getting paid only when you work?"

Imagine that you have thirty active business builders in your organization, each averaging a ten-hour-a-week part-time commitment to sign up new customers. That means you can, potentially, be paid on 300 hours of other people's efforts every single week–even if you're on vacation!

After your prospects understand the power of residual income, I recommend that you explain the compensation plan of your company. Always tailor your explanation to your audience. If you're presenting to an 80-year-old retired blue collar worker, I don't recommend that you talk about making a six-figure income. If you are presenting to a successful business owner, you shouldn't stop at the $400 a month level! Tailor your presentation to the particular person or audience before you, so each person can understand the full residual income potential of the opportunity.

Use visual aids with all prospects. Visual aids are important as you share numbers and percentages with your prospects.

Keep the compensation plan simple. If you make it sound complicated by talking about every bonus and every level, fewer people will sign up immediately. That will mean more follow-up work for you, and reduced probability of signing up each person. Wait until follow-up trainings, after the prospects have signed up, to go over the entire compensation plan and all the bonuses. In the initial presentation you're trying to get the prospect to see the power and potential of residual income, not explain it in its entirety.

When I present the compensation plan, I divide it into three main areas.

The first main area of interest is up-front promotional income. This income deals with up-front money that can be earned for selling packages, for enrolling new customers and recruiting new business builders. This will vary considerably among different companies. Some won't have such a plan at all, or it will be minimal.

The second part of the compensation plan deals with cash, car, revenue, profit and sometimes profit sharing, and house allowances. These types of bonuses are earned for moving up through the leadership levels.

The third part of the compensation program is residual income and the residual potential of earning lifetime income for going out and building a business with this company. After you go through these three streams of income, move to the last step of the presentation.

The last step of the presentation is the close.

These are a few sample closes I suggest that you use in your presentation.

"After everything you've heard about our products, our company and our compensation program, does this sound like a business you would like to get into to make some extra money, or does this sound like a good organization you would like to join so you can buy quality products at wholesale prices?"

In the close you always want to give a yes-yes response. "Do you want to be a customer or do you want to do the business?"

You never want to give a close like, "Well, after everything you have heard, do you want to do this or not?" That's called the yes-no close. It offers the prospect the opportunity to say, "No." And if they say, "No," then what will you do?

You want to make it a positive-positive close so that every person you present to will have a choice of two positive responses.

Not everybody that you present to will enroll, of course, but the likelihood of signing up a lot of people is very high with this kind of close.

Now, what you do *not* want to do (another common pitfall in ending the close), is to go over the whole presentation and then *not close*! You might be tempted to say, "Okay, you've heard all the information. Let me know what you think."

That's *really* bad! That's *a common pitfall*, which a lot of people fall into! You're giving your audience every opportunity to say, "No," *and not encouraging them to say, "Yes!"* You're not giving them even the *opportunity* of a positive response!

You *always* want to give a positive close and make a positive statement like, "Would you like to join as a customer or as a business builder?"

You always want to give that positive close. You always want to offer a choice between positive alternatives.

CHAPTER SEVEN

BUILD A MEGA-BUSINESS BY CLONING YOURSELF

Duplication is the skill of cloning yourself, your abilities, knowledge, work styles and motivation into other people in your organization. Duplication results from training every member of your organization to follow *exactly* the methods that have made you successful, and have been laid out by the company and your upline to guarantee success. This is true in any business, but it's *especially true and absolutely essential* in network marketing.

In other businesses, you'll encounter the person who does the work of two (or ten) people, and through such efforts becomes known for his or her success. If you look behind surface appearances, however, such a person is *either* limited by the number of hours in the day, no matter how efficiently and productively those hours are used, *or* that person has created unlimited potential by building a support network of people who are working in a similar manner, thus creating a more productive and efficient organization than would be possible if that person and everyone else were working on his or her own.

If you work on your own in network marketing you can make a modest income, but never more than that. If you build a network of *customers*, without developing any duplication (*business builders*), you'll soon run out of people readily willing to become customers. No matter how good you are, no matter how hard you work, no matter how creatively you market, you'll find it harder and harder to develop new customers. There is a limit to how far you can go.

This is not to minimize the importance of customers! They're vital! But without duplication and business builders, there is a limit to how far you can go.

Your business builders are the people who will fuel your success. Each customer they find adds to your income as well as theirs.

When I talk about duplicating yourself, I'm talking about finding and developing your business builders. When you train your business builder to achieve success the same way you have, you've cloned yourself. If you fail to clone yourself in this manner, your success will have a ceiling.

When you completely duplicate (clone) yourself, you've reached the point where your income becomes totally residual.

**"The cloning experiment has been a
complete failure."**

Your business now has the potential to grow by many customers without requiring much (if any) of your direct involvement. Your involvement in training the business builders to go forth and do what you've done, in the same way you did it, will produce skyrocketing income for you–and for them, as they clone themselves in the same manner you did.

Duplicating yourself is an ongoing process. It continues for many months, perhaps years. You're always looking for more business builders and training them to duplicate yourself. When you have sufficient duplication in your business, retirement, if you choose, is right around the corner.

Creating Duplication

The first step in creating duplication is finding the right people to work with. As I've said, not everyone will become a business builder. Most people who sign up will be customers. I look for certain traits in people I select to mentor. I want to work with people who will respond to my mentoring. If they don't, what's the point of working with them? When people respond to my mentoring (and yours), duplication will occur–and it will continue to occur.

The person must be coachable. The people you work with must understand that you have a proven system for success. They must bring a wide-open mind, a deep thirst for your knowledge, and leave their egos at the front door. This is the first quality to look for. Actually, people with really strong egos are the best kind. They're not insecure about themselves and don't need to challenge everything you try to teach, as someone with an insecure ego might. If a person doesn't listen when you coach, or challenges every proven technique you try to teach them, that person will not become a business builder. *Don't waste time on such people.*

Does the person have at least ten hours a week carved out to do this business? If you want to have a self-perpetuating business, and expect it to last for years to come, duplicating your efforts with a very part-time person is not a wise use of your time and energy, in most cases. (There are exceptions, but they're rare.) I spend most of my time working with aggressive full-time business builders and some part-time people who make up for their lack of time with skill and efficient, aggressive business-building.

Work with the willing. The duplication process requires that you and the new person both want this to happen. If you try to work with a person who really doesn't want to have a big business, this is obviously the wrong person to work with. Match their energy, enthusiasm and drive, but never exceed it. You cannot drag your people across the finish line. They must want to run to the finish and succeed by themselves. If their energy is sufficient to become customers, teach them how to be good customers, and leave it at that. Devote your real energy to people who want to become business builders.

Work with good quality people. If you were to start a clothing store in your town, it would be wise to hire a manager and sales people who have experience in retail clothing sales. The same is true with duplication in your business. It will likely take you more time to duplicate your skills working with a 65-year-old grandmother who has been a homemaker all of her life than it would to work with a 36-year-old sales rep who has won awards for sales performance for the last four years in a row.

Remember, anyone *can* duplicate successful techniques, but reality is that some *will*, some *won't*. In your limited time, you want the odds to be in your favor. You'll learn to identify the *"won'ts"* and will not waste time working with them.

Does your leader have good contacts? It is easier to duplicate signing up a lot of people if the person you're working with has a lot of personal contacts. Remember, with duplication, people will do what you do, not what you say. Work with this thought in mind. Every activity you do should be an activity you want to encourage others to replicate. If you find yourself doing activities that you don't want your business builders to duplicate, stop doing those non- or counter-productive activities.

Work with people who have a long-term attitude. Some people I worked with appeared to have all the potential in the world–but they wanted to make an unrealistic amount of money right away with limited time commitment. It was as if they thought all they had to do was sign up and they'd have instant wealth, sort of like you make instant coffee. It doesn't work that way, of course.

You need to remind your new business builders that in a typical business it takes three years or so to break even, and most fail to ever get into the black. You can make money in networking much sooner, and you're more certain to make money, but it still takes time to show results. Patience and persistence are the way to go. I would rather work with a less talented person who had an absolute five-year part-time commitment to become financially successful versus a real dynamo who wants to break all the records in the first three months working five hours a week.

Use your instincts and good judgment. The longer you are in business, the more you will understand that some will, some won't. So what? *Next*! You'll develop a 6th sense for who will duplicate your success and who is all talk and no action.

I encourage you to allow others in your upline who have more years of experience to help you judge who will be good. I've helped many hundreds in my business make the right decisions about who they should spend their time with. When you learn to spot those who will become successful business builders, use your knowledge to enhance the careers of the business builders *you* are working with!

Some key traits in a network marketer are time, desire, and commitment. A broad-based existing network, together with sales and business experience, is a plus, but not necessary. Plenty of people without sales or network experience have succeeded beyond their wildest dreams.

When I first started, I worked with anyone and everyone. As my business developed, I became more selective about who I was going to spend my time with. Remember that no matter how hard you work, no matter how efficiently you use your time, you only have a certain number of hours in any day when you can work your business. Don't waste them; use them wisely.

Your goal, eventually, is to work only with people who can be as good as, or potentially better, than you. However, in your first several months, try to duplicate yourself with anyone who remotely fits this profile. Don't forget that there are always exceptions to the rule. I have a 21-year-old college student earning $15,000 a month and a 68-year-old retired housewife doing nearly as well!

Before I talk about how to create duplication, I want to explain why it is such an essential part of building a large business. The larger your organization, the more critical it will become for duplication to become prevalent in your business because you can only do so much yourself. Networking is like team sports. One *great player* can impact the course of a game, but only *great teams* win championships. Only great teams, which constantly recruit and develop new rookies, continue to win championships.

When you have a few hundred customers in your business, it cannot continue to flourish if you haven't created duplication. Imagine a circus juggler spinning plates. He can only spin so many plates at one time before the plates come crashing to the ground. However, if this pro trained other people to spin plates with even only part of his or her precision, many times or more plates could be kept spinning at the same time. The more people he or she trains, the more plates can be spun.

Thus, to get beyond a hundred or so people in your business, if you want to create a large business and make it thrive, follow the duplication method I mentor to my organization.

The four steps to create duplication are:

First, help the person you identified as your potential future leader to set realistic goals, create a workable action plan, and have realistic expectations–and then start helping him or her to achieve those goals. It's important that new people set their own goals, but make sure the goals they set are realistic. Unrealistic goals are a guarantee of failure. Even if the business is really working for them, if they don't achieve an unrealistic goal, they'll feel as if they failed–when they were actually succeeding and on the road to greater success! But if they *believe* they failed–they're failures. *Perception* of failure–or success–is just as important as reality, and sometimes more so.

A motto I use when I mentor is: "Underestimate and over-deliver."

An action plan is a written-down agenda of what the new person needs to do each week to accomplish the goals that have been set. Once you've assisted in this process, which was covered in greater detail in an earlier chapter, the big first step in duplication is to work with the person. Another phrase I use in working with a new person is "Lock onto a new person like a pit bull." The more you are around this person, the better.

In order to create duplication, you need to do group meetings for this person's guests, do two-on-ones for the person, see each other socially, drive to appointments together, talk on the phone at least daily to go over the day's production, introduce the new person to other leaders in the area, be in regular and consistent contact with the person and his or her three best people, and take this person with you to meetings you do.

Practice makes perfect. Thus, in step one, formulate a plan and be with this new person as many hours as you can each week so your enthusiasm, work ethic, and skills can rub off!

The second step is to teach your business builders how to do the phone invitation and learn the art of overcoming objections.

In order to duplicate success, you must duplicate the seeds all successful people plant in their networking gardens. What I do in my mentoring is threefold. First, after the new business builder has his or her written list of at least 100 prospects, I help categorize the list into three areas:

1. The chicken list, i.e. the people her or she is too chicken to call but who would be great at the business
2. Potential business builders
3. Potential customers

Once the list is categorized, we practice the phone invitation together. This includes role-playing techniques for overcoming common objections, and teaching the three major telephone approaches: the different techniques for dealing with those on his or her chicken list, those who have been identified as potential business builders, and those who will probably be customers. I recommend you spend at least an hour or so role playing.

Take turns role playing both sides of the conversation. The two avenues are when you are the prospect being invited, and when you are business builder inviting the new person. In Chapter Eight you will learn many invitation techniques.

The formula is: phone calls = appointments = sign ups = growth in your customer base and your income.

So far, you have set up the new person's business, taught invitation and presentation skills, and duplicated this with a hands-on approach. It is very difficult to teach duplication over the phone or through the fax or mail. Networking is a people business. Thus, remote-control shortcuts usually produce less than adequate results in the duplication process.

Remember that you only have to duplicate yourself a few times to earn many years of residual income, so it is worth your time to hand-hold these business builders for at least the first few months.

A good analogy, perhaps, is your family. An average family has two to three children. I am sure you would agree that it is necessary and fulfilling to guide your children as they learn to walk, talk, become toilet-trained, feed themselves, start school, run, ride a bike, have friends, drive, date, graduate, get married and eventually start their own families so you can spoil your grandchildren and continue your family tradition. This requires a lot of time and money, but it's what most of us live for.

In networking, the better teacher, mentor, and duplicator you are, teaching the correct principles of building a business, the more fulfilling and lucrative your pay-off will be!

The third step in the successful duplication process arises from your belief and commitment, and the teamwork you display.

Remember that people will *do what you do, not what you say*. It is very important to duplicate your *belief* in your networking business. If your belief in the product/services/compensation plan is strong, your organization will be strong and never falter.

These are the items you should–and should not–display to your organization to show them the strength of your personal belief in your company and your system:

In your house, use *all* of the products/services your company markets. Do not use competing brands.

Display a list of your goals on the walls of your home office.

Show your daily planner to your new business builders, demonstrating that during your hours of commitment to grow your business, you are setting and doing appointments.

Always talk positively about everything your company represents.

When you are down in the dumps, call your upline. Do not spread your problems down-line; this will weaken their belief.

Do what you say. Be a person of your word. If you abide by this principle, you will have many committed followers. Before you say or do anything in front of your new business builder, ask yourself if you would like these things duplicated.

Be a role model.

Do not exaggerate or lie. This will weaken the bonds and beliefs of your business builders in you.

Always conduct your activities in ways people will look up to and admire.

Keep enrolling new people.

Lead by example.

Tell them true product stories that show what using the products or services has done for people.

Create a price comparison sheet to show that your company's prices are better than the competition.

Get members of your organization together with other successful leaders in your company when possible. Success rubs off when people are consistently exposed to it.

Be a humble leader, not a know-it-all, so people will believe they can duplicate you. If you brag about extraordinary goals, incomes, talents, or results relating to *anything* you have done, past or present, the belief your new people have that they can duplicate you will diminish–even if what you are saying is true.

Always try to relate to the person you are mentoring. Even if your intentions are the best possible, talking over his or her head lowers that person's belief in himself or herself. Remember that raised belief = raised long-term income = results for your new business builders. I can't over-emphasize the importance of making sure your people *believe* in you and in themselves, and in their *realistic* goals.

Your commitment and the teamwork you show to your business is very important to the duplication process. Every possible appointment and three-way call you go on will show your commitment to being a team player and will rub off geometrically. Return all phone calls within 24 hours, *especially* to business builders you are working with closely.

In creating duplication, you also need to work with your people's people–those whom your business builders are bringing in. This commitment to "driving the lines deep" is a fundamental necessity to create long-term duplication.

Remember that each new business builder you are mentoring is a unique individual and most likely isn't capable of working effectively with their new people yet. If you show your commitment to them by teaming up with their new business builders, this will strengthen your business and the duplication process.

The last step toward successful duplication is making each of your new business builders a good teacher. They wouldn't have succeeded if you were not a good teacher; their new business builders won't succeed unless you've taught them to be good teachers.

This means getting your business builders to do for their good people what you did for them.

The easiest way to teach your business builders to teach duplication is for your training system to be easily duplicatable. In designing your training, presentation and follow-up procedures, ask yourself these questions:

Is it simple to understand?

Can the average person duplicate the information?

Can it be taught by your business builders in the future?

A good coach, teacher or mentor will always be able to say yes to these questions. Your goal is to duplicate yourself into as many people as possible, and to have these people duplicate the same principles to their groups. This is the fastest and easiest way to create a large business.

In summary, the benefits of duplication are:

1. **Leverage:** The ability to have others you trained grow their businesses and yours at the same time without your direct involvement; i.e., your business grows even while you aren't working.

2. **Leadership:** Duplication creates leadership. The benefit is twofold.

    (A) If new people coming into your business see a broad base of leadership in their area, rather than just one guru, their confidence in believing they can succeed will increase.

    (B) This creates long-term stability in your income, which you will see during months you are not working as hard.

3. **Large potential income and customer growth**. John Paul Getty, the first billionaire in this country, said it best. He said, "I would rather have 1% of 100 people's efforts than 100% of my own effort."

4. **Longevity in your business and income.** With duplication, you create the fuel necessary to continue to propel your business vehicle to prosperity.

5. **Lifetime retirement**. If you create massive duplication in your business, the potential for you to retire with an

income that can sustain the quality of life you desire will occur as a natural result of your duplication. Some of the people I have mentored have retired in their 30s and 40s with a six-figure income, because we teamed up to create massive duplication.

CHAPTER EIGHT
ALL THE WORLD'S
A STAGE–
BUT BE SURE TO
REHEARSE AT HOME!

In Chapter Five I gave you the basic steps of how to invite a new business builder or customer. *This is one of the most essential skills for getting off to a good start and continuing to grow your business.* Because this is so important, for this chapter I asked three successful business builders to join me and show you how to present the invitation.

The balance of this chapter will be *role playing*. Joe Tore, Paul Kupetsky, and Denise Harris will be inviting each other the way they would invite their friends, family, acquaintances, strangers, and referrals. They have 40 years of combined experience, and are some of our industries best prospectors.

You can use this information to practice your inviting skills, and to invite your contacts.

Role Playing: How to Invite Prospects and Overcome Objections

Paul Kupetsky begins:

Paul: Thanks, Russ, we really appreciate the opportunity to help new people learn how to invite. Denise Harris, Joe Tore and I have gone through the same beginning steps that your readers are taking now. We'd like to help your readers through those steps by going through some scenarios and reliving some phone conversations we've had.

Joe: I'd like to give you an example of how I call up a friend. You can learn your inviting skills by talking to people you know. They'll forgive you if you aren't perfect–and you won't be, at first. When I got into my business, the first thing I did was call people I knew. I called a friend who was very successful, someone who had been a friend in high school, to whom I hadn't spoken to in a long time. So let me jump into it. Paul will take the role of my friend.

Ring, ring.

Paul: Hello.

Joe: Hello, Paul. This is Joseph Tore. I don't know if you remember me, but we went to school together. Remember when we had Mrs. Bigelow in 12th grade? I was the skinny, good-looking guy. How are you doing, buddy, good? What have you been doing with yourself? Listen, Paul, I'd love to catch up on old times, but I called for a specific reason. This is completely about business. I'll catch up later. Do you have a minute? Paul, I recently got involved with an unbelievable business opportunity. It has absolutely changed my life. I haven't spoken to you in a long time, but you're one of the first people I thought of. I was hoping to schedule a few minutes of your time–about thirty-five to forty-five minutes–to sit down with you and show you the basic facts, and why and how some of the partners I'm working with are generating a substantial income, part time. This will really get you excited. I can either meet you...

Paul: Can you give me more details?

Joe: I can give you *tons* of detail. I can do it on Thursday, or Friday if that's a better day for you.

153

Paul: Let me look at my schedule. It may be the right place, right time in my life, too. I've been looking to do other things, so the timing is good. Thursday would be great.

Joe: I could do it during the day–or would the evening be better for you?

Paul: It'll be good to see you again.

Joe: I can't wait. It's going to be such a ball. Did you say day or evening?

Paul: Evening.

Joe: I'll put you down for Thursday evening. Would seven o'clock be good for you?

Paul: 7:30 would be better.

Joe: I'm putting you on my schedule for 7:30. Shall I hold while you put it in your schedule?

Paul: Do you want Denise here, too?

Joe: Paul, you're married! Congratulations! Things have really changed!

Paul: We have a baby, too.

Joe: That's wonderful! If Denise can be there, that will be great! She'll probably ask questions you and I might not think of. I'm putting you down for 7:30. If anything comes up between now and then that might stop us from meeting, please call me at least two days in advance. That will give me a chance to re-book my schedule and make sure my whole day doesn't fall apart.

Paul: I don't see anything coming up.

Joe: So you'll call me two days in advance?

Paul: Sure.

Joe: Fantastic, Paul! I'm excited about meeting you.

Paul: Me too! Take care.

(End of call.)

Paul: That was an easy one. That was someone who was receptive. You love it when you get that kind of response. If you make enough calls, you'll find that's going to happen, but most of the time you get more resistence. It isn't just making the calls; it's *making the calls with the right approach*. The **number one reason** for lack of success in this business is a poor approach. *This is very important!* Your ability to approach people successfully will determine your level of success! In the beginning, you need to work with your partners so that you can learn the right approach. *You* have to learn it first! *Then* you can teach it. *Then* it is duplicatable.

When you use the right approach, 7 percent of your effectiveness is the words, 38 percent in your voice inflection or the excitement in your voice, and 55 percent will be the passion you show. What I got on the phone with my friends, I knew what they wanted. I knew Joe was looking for a BMW. He always wanted a BMW. He always talked about a BMW. Every time he saw a BMW, he said, "Paul, look at that BMW!" So was I going to talk to Joe about a Chevy? No! This is the conversation I had with Joe:

Ring, ring.

Joe: Hello.

155

Paul: Joe, it's Paul. You are not going to believe this! I found a way for you to get that BMW. Joe, I found a way to– *(CLICK!)*

Joe: Hello? Paul? He hung up on me! Well, let me get his number.

Ring, ring.

Joe: Hello, Paul.

Paul: Joe, I'm so sorry. I don't even know what I'm doing. Joe, what are you doing right now? Joe, this is like nothing you have ever seen! I'm so excited! I'm going to talk to everybody about it! I know a BMW is what you've talked about; that's all you wanted. I'm coming over. Put a pot of coffee on. I'll be there in about ten minutes.

Joe: He hung up on me again!

(End of call.)

Paul: I never waited for anybody to give me an excuse. You can do this with close friends. ***Don't do this with strangers! It doesn't work***!

Joe: I'd like to give you an example of how sometimes things don't go perfectly. Some of the best people I've been able to get into my organization didn't just say, "Hey, that sounds great! I'm in! Where do I sign?" Bringing them into my organization took persistence on my part. I kept after them, month after month. I'd like to give you an example of a guy named Oscar. We'd been in a home-based business together before. We both lost money so I didn't have a tremendous amount of credibility in his eyes. This example gives an idea of how a telephone invitation to a resistant prospect goes.

Ring, ring.

Joe: Hello. Yes, is Oscar in?

Oscar: You're talking to Oscar.

Joe: Oscar, how're you doing? This is Joseph Tore.

Oscar: Oh, no!

Joe: Don't worry, Oscar. You're not speaking to me, still?

Oscar: It's okay.

Joe: I just wanted to give you a call.

Oscar: I like you, Joe. It's just that we had a bad experience.

Joe: We both had the same experience. It was bad for both of us. We each know it was bad for many people. You know, I just wanted to say that it was an experience and a tremendous education. If nothing else, I really learned what *not* to do. Oscar, I'm going to ask you to not throw away all that time and education, because somebody recently put a business opportunity across my desk that is *unbelievable*. And I promise you, Oscar, *this one is not a scam!* There is *no* inventory loading. There is *no* big dollar investment. There's *no* retailing, *no* taking orders, and there are *no* big volume requirements.

Oscar: So?

Joe: I want to tell you something, Oscar. This company has been in business for thirteen years and has grown as a company each year.

Oscar: You're talking....

Joe: I know. That's what I want to do. I want to have the opportunity to sit down with you for about forty-five minutes and put that information in front of you, show you the facts and exactly why people, month after month, year after year, are reordering what this company provides. It will blow your mind.

Oscar: I'm just getting my life back. I've got a job. I'm doing well. I was very close to losing my house, *very close to losing my family!* Joe, you've never reached any level of success. What credibility do you have? What are you making in this?

Joe: That's a very good question. Let me start by saying this: If I had an opportunity that was like one of those schemes where people are getting hurt, where they're losing their money and only a few people on top are making all the money, if that's what I had to show you right now, *there is no way I'd be calling!* There's no way I'd get away with it if I did. You've been through that, just like I have. I'm *not* trying to get you into one of those. This is a different kind of business opportunity. It is the first and only one of its kind. People at the top, at the bottom, in the middle, just people across the board, average people, are winning. I just recently got involved. I don't have a lot to show for my involvement yet, but I'm in the black after my first month in the business. I'm *already* making money! I know you'd love this business.

Oscar: Joe, your timing is really off. I hear this all the time. You know how many calls I get because of my exposure in that other business? You're probably the twentieth call–if not more–I've gotten.

Joe: I can understand that, Oscar. Maybe you could do me a favor. I've been working at this opportunity and already, as I mentioned, things are going well. I'm seeing the results that we worked so hard over the years to get, but maybe you can give me your opinion. Just try and plunch some holes in this and just see if

you can find something I missed. I would really appreciate it and
I promise you...

Oscar: You know what would happen if I even *considered*
this? My wife would kill me. I put her through a lot with the other
business. Right now, the timing is not right for me.

Joe: Is your wife home? Maybe you can get her on the phone.
She should be there when we meet.

Oscar: Joe, I don't think so.

Joe: Let me end with this before I let you go. I'm sure you'd
still be open to doubling your income. You're still interested in
making more money, aren't you?

Oscar: Absolutely! That's not the question. The question is,
what am I going to do with my time *this* time?

Joe: Are you considering at least taking that forty-five minutes
to hear me out, to see why so many people are winning? Would
you give me 45 minutes Tuesday, or maybe Thursday?

Oscar: Joe, you're persistent. Don't get obnoxious.

Joe: Oscar, thank you anyway. I do appreciate the time you've
given me, but before I hang up, at least allow me this much. Can
I keep the channels open? Will you allow me to give you a call in
the next couple of months to update you on my progress in this
business and kind of let you know where I'm at?

Oscar: I have no problem with that. I've always liked you.

Joe: I feel the same. I'll speak to you over the next few
months.

(End of call.)

Joe: Remember, folks, you are going to get no's. *If you're not getting no's, you are not doing the business.* This is just an example of what it takes to get your best people.

Now Denise will show us how she approached a family member.

Denise: One of the scenarios I come across a lot involves people who have joined my business who have successful people in their families, for example a brother who's a business owner. They would really like to have their relative take a look at this opportunity. They know what their relative's capabilities are, business-wise, but it really makes them nervous to talk business with them–particularly those who are more successful than themselves. In this situation, I like to go with the opinion approach, the "I'd value your input," approach.

Ring, ring, ring.

Denise: Hi, Richie.

Richie: Denise?

Denise: Yup. Your favorite sister. How are you doing? Listen, Richie, on a serious note...

Richie: How serious?

Denise: Pretty serious. I'm only going to take a minute of your time, but I need your help, Richie. I want you to take a look at something. I've recently had a great business concept come across my desk, and I'm telling you this really makes a lot of sense. I know you have all kinds of business experience, and I really want you to take a look at this. I can't punch a hole in it. I want you to look at it.

Richie: Denise, you are not asking me to get involved in anything, are you? You know my schedule.

Denise: I know how busy you are! That's *exactly* why I'm calling you, as a matter of fact. I see this as something designed for busy people. If you want to get involved, that's great. If you don't want to get involved, that's great, too, but your input is really important to me here. Another thing is, even if you choose not to get involved, when you see how good it is I know you're going to be more than happy to refer me to people who might be interested, because you network all the time. You know all kinds of people. I know this would be perfect for some of them.

Richie: Denise, for you I'll look at it. Don't ask me to do it, but I'll look at it for you. If I think it's good, I'll let tell you. If I can punch holes in it, you'd better believe I'll punch holes! That's what you're looking for, right? My opinion? When do you want to see me?

Denise: What are you doing tomorrow night? Are you going to be at Mom's house?

Richie: Yeah, I'll be at Mom's.

Denise: Okay, after dinner we'll sit down. But you have to be serious. You have to listen to this. You have to give me an open, honest opinion, but you have to let me explain everything.

Richie: You'll have my total attention. I give you my best opinion, you can be sure of that.

Denise: Okay, honey, see you tomorrow night.

(End of call.)

Paul: I do a lot of warm referrals, that is, people referred by others who they think are likely prospects. They are usually 90 to 95 percent sold before I start, because if the person I got the name from has credibility, it's usually an easy presentation to close. I 'm going to take you through an example of that kind of call. I'm going to call Joe, who has been referred by Bob.

Ring, ring.

Joe: Hello.

Paul: Joe, you don't know me. My name is Paul Kupetsky. You were referred by Bob Daniels. He spoke very highly of you.

Joe: I don't know any Bob Daniels.

Paul: Well, he knows you. He said that you're a terrific person. He said you work well with people, you're very busy, very successful and you might be open for an opportunity. Let me give you a little background. We're looking for people who are successful at what they do and who are busy. We're a group of professional and business people who have learned to diversify. We put our time into a company that pays us on a residual basis. Let me tell you what this isn't. This *is not* a scam. I want to clear the air on that. This *is not* illegal. We wouldn't do that to you! I'm calling because you were highly recommended. I only work from referrals. I'd like to set up an appointment to go over some of the numbers with you. I know you're busy. I'm busy, too. The bottom line is I need about thirty to forty-five minutes of your undivided attention. Could we meet for coffee or lunch? What's good for you? Days, evenings, weekends?

Joe: I think you're jumping the gun. It was Paul, right?

Paul: Yes.

Joe: I can appreciate everything you've said and I appreciate the compliments from this guy I know, but why don't you tell me a little bit about it. I'm very busy and I'd appreciate a little more information now.

Paul: Absolutely. Let me give you some background. You're a director of marketing? That was my background, too. I did that for many years. I had no time. I didn't even have time to turn around! A good friend introduced me to this business. He told me it was for busy people. I turned him down. I said, "Randy, I'm just too busy!" But he became very successful and earned a great income in his first year. His lifestyle was as busy as mine, if not even busier, so I took another look at it–and boy, am I glad I did! All I'm asking you to do is take a look at it. I'm not asking you to make a decision now. You don't have a right to say no until you sit down with me. We're a company out of the West Coast. We're growing fast, but we're being careful not to try to grow *too* fast! We're looking for business people who can pool some of their time with us. Some of us put in three to five hours a week, some five to ten, some ten to fifteen, but the bottom line, the only reason I'm on the phone with you, Joe, is that I think you can do really well for yourself with this company–and that you can contribute to the company's growth, which will benefit you, me, and everyone involved.

Joe: Um-hum.

Paul: We don't call just anybody. We go by referrals. I know you have a lot of questions, but that's why we have to get together. I am not after money. We're well capitalized. There is no selling, no inventory, no paperwork. There is no rah-rah. This is a *business*. I'd like to make an appointment with you. You make the decision. How is during the week for you? Is that better, or would you prefer a night or weekend appointment?

Joe: Wednesday might be good. Why don't you give me a call Wednesday morning? I'll let you know if that works out for me.

Paul: Let me put it to you this way. I'm also very busy. My time is valuable, just like yours. I need to lock in a time to meet. Why don't you look at your calendar and let's see if we can pull some time together and lock it in. If there's a change, you can always give me some notice and I can change my schedule, but at this point I need to know exactly the time.

Joe: Let me see, six o'clock, you said.

Paul: That will work.

Joe: Six o'clock is good. I'll put it in my schedule.

Paul: You have it in pen?

Joe: I have it in pen.

Paul: Good, because mine is in pen, too. Let me give you my pager number. If something comes up, please give me a call so I can reschedule.

Joe: Absolutely. I'm looking forward to the appointment.

Paul: Same here.

(End of call.)

Joe: That's a great way of using a referral by just letting people know that they were spoken of highly. I'd like to give you another scenario where I call Paul, a small business owner I know. I'm going to try to take advantage of getting both Paul and his wife on the phone, because I feel that if you get the appointment with just one person, you encounter the problem of the other person not having heard what was said and agreed to in the phone conversation and canceling the appointment because something else came up or they don't want to talk with you.

Ring, ring.

Joe: Hello, Paul.

Paul: Yes.

Joe: How you doing, buddy? This is Joe Tore. I was wondering if you have a few minutes.

Paul: Absolutely.

Joe: Listen, Paul, I recently got involved in a business. I'd like you to get your wife on the phone, so you can both hear about this. Is Denise home?

Paul: She's right here.

Joe: Would you ask her to pick up the extension?

Paul: Denise, pick up the other phone. It's Joe Tore. He wants to talk to you about something.

Joe: Hello, Denise, how are you? How's everything going? Listen, Denise, I know this is unusual, but I wanted to talk to both you guys. I know we haven't seen each other in a couple of weeks, but let me just give it to you straight. Some partners have recently put a business venture across my desk which is unbelievable. It's based in the West, and has recently come into this region. The income is solid, it's lucrative, it's unreal, and people like you and I, across the country, are already starting to generate income. The guys who showed us this are doing phenomenally well.

165

Paul: Joe, you know our time constraints. Denise, this sounds a little bit like...

Denise: I know, you know what it is. I have to tell you Joe, we were just discussing money and we're really not doing as well as we expected in our business.

Joe: Let me stop you now and save you some time. I'm *not* looking for investors, or for people's money. I'm not looking for your credit cards or bank accounts. I'm looking for people like you who are too busy to go out and start another business, too busy to get a third job, but who can really use an extra $500, $1,000, $2,000, $5,000, or maybe even more, per month.

Paul: How are you going to do it?

Joe: This business is custom-made for the busy person. It's based on leverage. If you guys weren't busy, if you were sitting home watching reruns of the Brady Bunch, I wouldn't call you.

Paul: Is this one of those scams?

Joe: No, no, no.

Denise: Oh, please, not again!

Joe: You guys mean like an illegal pyramid scheme?

Denise: Absolutely.

Joe: You're thinking you have to go to the big hype meetings and you have to buy inventory and take orders. Right?

Paul: We still have the box of tapes....

Denise: From *both* companies, Paul.

Joe: We don't do any of that stuff. It's not a scam. I'll guarantee you one thing. Give me forty-five minutes to let me show you exactly what it is and what it is not, and I guarantee it won't be a waste of your time. Does that sound fair?

Denise: Okay. Paul and I will look at it.

Joe: Is nine PM Wednesday a good time?

Denise: That's fine. We'll see you then. Thanks, Joe.

(End of call.)

Joe: When you are out and about in your normal everyday world, always keep looking for prospects. Some people are better than others at striking up conversations with strangers, but everyone can learn how. It's just a matter of overcoming your own reticence about doing so, and working on the skill. When you do this, you have only one goal: *get the person's phone number*.

Paul: Any time I'm out and about, where I can talk to people, I may, for example, be shopping for clothes or groceries, but *I'm also shopping for prospects*. You have to understand that there are *suspects* and there are *prospects*. When they open their mouths, you know who the prospects are. With *suspects*, you practice your conversation-staring skills—and every so often they'll turn into prospects. When you find prospects, you get their telephone numbers.

The trick is to find someone you can talk to and give them a reason to talk to you. People love to help others, so I give them the opportunity to help me.

For example, one day when I was in the produce department at my grocery store, I saw a woman who looked sharp, self-possessed and confident. I asked her how to tell whether a melon was ripe. From that "can you help me" opening question we struck up a conversation, I learned she was in marketing, which was just the

167

kind of person I was looking for, and we developed enough rapport in that relatively brief conversation to exchange business cards (which, of course, have phone numbers on them) and I had the opportunity to follow up with her.

Another time, I was at a gas station filling up my car–something as completely routine as grocery shopping–and saw a guy at the next pump filling up a blue Buick that looked like the kind of car Waldbaum's Supermarkets provides for their managers. I figured anybody who was a Waldbaum's manager would be a good prospect, so I got a conversation going–and discovered that he had no idea that Waldbaum's supermarkets provides cars like his to their managers. He was a dentist, so I knew how to approach him. I got the phone number and followed up.

Both these examples are contacts that worked because I wasn't afraid to start a conversation, and the other person read me as sincere and responded. Perhaps the next few dozen women in supermarkets or guys at gas stations wouldn't have responded, but if I had not started those conversations, and many more that produced no results at all, I would not have made those contacts.

That's why you should work on your conversation-starting skills. You'll find that as you get better at making presentations to prospects who agree to meet with you, you'll also develop better conversation-starting skills and will lose your fear of talking to strangers. As you get better at phone follow up and making presentations, these conversation-starting skills will also develop and become more natural. After a while, you'll wonder why you ever thought it was hard. Remember, always, that you'll talk to a lot of people for every person who responds, and of those who respond, some will turn down your offer, some will only become customers–but a certain number will become business builders. As Russ has said many times in this book, networking is a numbers game!

Some of you may have a comic strip called *The Norm* in your local newspaper. One of the recurring themes in it is that Norm borrows a neighbor's dog to take for a walk in the park, hoping to meet women who love dogs. The result is always something hilarious. One time, the dog led Norm to all his ex-girlfriends! That was a real hoot–but don't laugh too hard. One technique I sometimes use when I want to make contacts is to go to the park with my dog's leash, but I leave the dog at home. I pretend to be looking for the dog. Sometimes that results in a contact and a conversation.

What I'm saying is that whatever works for you as conversation-starter, use it! Always be alert for someone with whom you can start a conversation, who might be interested in networking.

Joe: Let me ask you a question, Paul. In scenarios where we go up and talk to someone we've never met, what if I were an insurance agent? What would you tell me?

Paul: I help insurance agents and other professionals develop multiple incomes.

Joe: What if I was a mortgage broker?

Paul: I help mortgage brokers and other professionals develop multiple incomes. I can't promise you anything.

Joe: What if I were a school teacher?

Paul: I help school teachers and other professionals develop multiple incomes.

Denise: What if I were a stay-at-home mom?

Paul: I help stay-at-home moms earn extra income on a part-time basis without giving up the time you need for your family. This is a walk-away income. We're so excited about this!

Joe: Let's run a scenario of how a follow-up call to someone you met like this might go. Paul, suppose I met you last week,

169

when you were the salesman I talked to while shopping at Sears. I got your card and promised to follow up.

Ring, ring.

Joe: Hello, is Paul in?

Paul: Paul speaking.

Joe: Paul, hi, this is Joe Tore. I don't know if you remember me. I talked to you last week when I was shopping at Sears. I got your business card. I was the guy with the marketing company, remember?

Paul: Yeah, how are you doing?

Joe: I'm doing great. Listen, I wanted to give you a call, like I promised I would. I'm sorry I didn't get in touch with you sooner. Things have just been exploding.

Paul: It sounded interesting.

Joe: Do you have a few minutes for me now? Great! Paul, I recently got involved in a business that has absolutely changed my life. It's helping people all across the country generate a second income without jeopardizing their present income. I think it's something you'd be great at. I'd love to set an appointment with you for sometime in the next few days, put some information in front of you, and show you exactly how and why people like you and me are generating such substantial incomes, part-time. I could do it Wednesday or Thursday. What would be better for you?

Paul: I'll be honest with you, Joe, I have no time.

Joe: Paul, I completely understand that. That was my biggest problem when I took a look at this the first time. I was so busy I didn't know where I would fit it in, but this business is custom-made for busy people. It's based on leverage. If you don't have time, that's *exactly* why you need to sit down and take a look at this. It will give you more time to do things you don't have time to do now. I can do it on Thursday or would Friday be better?

Paul: Okay, why don't we? Could you give me a little more information before we sit down? Could you send me some information?

Joe: I'll do better than that. I'll *hand deliver it* and walk you through it. Let me give you a little background. It's a company based in the West. I think I mentioned that when I first met you. It's a company that did millions in sales last year. *Unbelievable!* It's new in your area. I'll explain more of the details when we get together. It's a visual presentation. Did you say Wednesday was good, or is Thursday better?

Paul: I don't know. Do I *have to* get people involved? Is this a....

Joe: There are a lot of different capacities in which you could do this business. Like any business, you need customers. Don't try and generalize and try to envision this as something you think it might be. It is like nothing you have ever seen. I promise, Paul, I'll explain everything when we get together. I guarantee it won't be a waste of your time.

Paul: What about investment?

Joe: There's virtually no investment. We are not looking for people's money, credit cards or life savings. We are just looking for good, hard-working people who want to generate a few extra thousand, $4,000, $5000, whatever they need, on a very part-time basis. I think it's something you'll love, but I can't make any promises. When I get together with you, I'll show you everything.

(Joe sets appointment and ends the phone call.)

Paul: What Joe has done is answered the objections. There were a bunch in this call–and that's not uncommon. What I like to do in the beginning of the conversation is answer the five things that are on the prospect's mind:

1. What is it?
2. If it is so great, why share it?
3. Why me?
4. How much money do I have to invest?
5. Is it a scam?

If you don't answer those objections early in the conversation, they plague the prospect, who keeps worrying about them after the call is done. The result is that many times the prospect doesn't show up, or you get cancellations because fear comes as a direct result of unanswered questions. Prospects begin to believe that it has to be one of those scams or phony investment deals, *and you lose them.*

You must answer *all the objections* and get a *firm appointment.*

Denise: We try to keep expanding our contact list. We're always adding people who are just acquaintances but not really friends, or maybe people you don't hang out with at night but maybe you work with them. Maybe you see them at the bus stop. What I'd like to do is show everybody how to approach somebody you work with. I think that is a very common scenario for a brand new business builder.

Ring, ring.

Denise: Hi, Paul, it's Denise.

Paul: Hi, Denise, how are you?

Denise: How're you doing?

Paul: How are the kids?

Denise: You are not used to my calling you at home, are you?

Paul: No. I'm used to meeting you at the bus stop and at work.

Denise: Listen, Paul. I only have a minute. I'm running out the door, but I've been meaning to call you kind of privately for the past couple of days because I have something I want to tell you about. I didn't really want to talk about it at work.

Paul: Sounds exciting, Denise.

Denise: It is! I'm *very* excited! Remember when we were in the cafeteria the other day and you were talking about not having enough money to send Ken to private school and how you guys are struggling a little bit?

Paul: We're looking at a lot of things. My wife is looking at stuffing envelopes. I'm looking at some computer things.

Denise: Never mind those things! My husband and I have come across this opportunity and we've been able to generate a *very* nice part-time income. Paul, I want to share it with you. I can choose to work with people I like in this business–and I like you.

Paul: I appreciate that. We're actively looking, like I said, but I don't want to get involved in one of those pyramid things.

Denise: I wouldn't be on the phone with you if it was one of *those*. I think you know me well enough to know that I'm not the type of person to pursue one of those things. This *really works!* I

173

want to share it with you because I care about you. It's okay if you say no, but I think by the end of the night you'll really be thanking me. I'm serious. I want to sit down with you and your wife.

Paul: Well, we're looking now, so we're open.

Denise: Hey, the worst you can do is take a look, see it and say, 'No, it's not for us,' but I'm telling you, it *is* going to be for you. We're going to have a lot of fun building a nice income together.

Paul: It sounds great, Denise. Thanks.

(End of call.)

Paul: As a conversation-starting guide, we use **FORM,** which Russ talked about earlier.

Family
Occupation
Recreation
Money

Somewhere in those four key hot buttons you're going to find some pain somewhere in almost anyone's life. When they tell you their pain, you say, "You know, I can't promise you anything, but if you hate your job, I may be able to help you."
Or, "Oh, you want your wife to be home with the kids? Gee, I can't promise you anything, but I may be able to help you."
Or, "You have children going to college? Gee, I can't promise you anything, but I may be able to help you."

Joe: I'd like to take this back to one thing. Follow-up is the key. *Absolutely* the key. I made a call, I think we said two months ago, to a guy named Oscar. He had tried a home-based business before, and was really burnt out. He didn't want to hear from me.

174

Ring, ring.

Oscar: Hello.

Joe. Hello, Oscar? Hey, buddy, how're you doing, It's Joe Tore. It's your monthly call. How's it going?

Oscar: A lot better, Joe, a lot better.

Joe: I'm glad to hear that. Hey, listen. I don't want to take too much of your time. I promised I'd give you a call and I didn't want to break my promise.

Oscar: Joe, you're the most persistent person I know.

Joe: Well, thank you. I appreciate that. I learned persistence from my girlfriend, watching her go out and build our business together.

Oscar: At least you're not obnoxious.

Joe: Well, thank you. I appreciate that, too. You should get to know me a little better before you make that assumption. Oscar, you know the reason I'm calling. I want to see if the timing is better. You asked me a question the last time I called. you. You said, how are you doing? What kind of success have you seen? Well, I know what you've been going through. I know the things we've lost money in before, but you have to get together with me, Oscar. You *are not going to believe* the results I've gotten from this business. Not with just a few people at the top, but with everybody! You won't *believe* what people are getting out of this business. It's so amazing you're going to make me prove it to you! But I'll do that. I need forty-five minutes of your time. If there is any way, Oscar, that you will sit down with me and do that, I guarantee you'll be glad you did.

Oscar: The only thing that's piqued my interest is that you keep reiterating that you and a lot of others are making money. But if I say "no," I don't want you to be hurt or anything. I've been there, done it, seen it.

Joe: I don't need you to say yes. Unless you really want to do this I would rather you just said "no," but I want you to know what you are saying no to. Look, we've all been burned, but no company that I've ever seen has a better cure for burns than this one. Give me forty-five minutes. Let me show you the facts and I guarantee you, Oscar, you'll *love* this. Does that sound fair?

Oscar: Yes, it does. I'll give you forty-five minutes, but that's it, forty-five minutes.

Joe: That's all I'll need.

(End of call.)

Denise: There are people out there who will say no to you permanently. You have to understand that. It is all part of the territory. All of us can say we've had people who just won't sit down with us.

Paul: *Never give up!* Ask yourself some questions every single day: "What did I do today to help my business? Did I talk to anybody? Did I make a phone call? Did I set an appointment? Did I do an appointment?" Keep an eye on those questions.

Russ: What powerful information these three people I've mentored have given you today. Like most of life's challenges, practice will make your skills in doing this business perfect on your inviting skills. I recommend that after reading this chapter, you practice these skills by getting on the phone.
Picture yourself making $10 every time you pick up the phone, and $30 each time you invite a contact, even if you aren't

successful at getting the appointment. The calls which result in new customers and business builders will pay you for every call in which you are turned down. Thus, you make money in the process of prospecting, not just when you get an appointment. Keep your head up, and keep making phone calls.

Good luck setting all the appointments you can. You will find that the more you do it, the more money you will make and the better you will become.

In Chapter Nine, I will be interviewing some of the most successful people I have ever partnered up with and mentored. They will teach you all the skills they've learned from hundreds of combined years in the networking Industry.

Get ready to learn from many six-figure-income earners!

CHAPTER NINE

THE PALEY TAPES: ON-THE-RECORD INTERVIEWS WITH SUCCESSFUL NETWORKERS

Interview #1:

Russ: Greg and Sheri Lagana live in Holmdel, New Jersey. We've been working together for seven years. They are the most successful people I've directly enrolled. Over the last seven years they've built a business of over 6,000 customers from the New Jersey area. Their business has generated an income of over $2.5 million.

I asked them what activities they do on a daily basis that have brought them to this level of success.

Greg: Prospecting is where it began; finding people we could eventually cold-call. We started with people who had home-based business experience, especially any type of multilevel marketing experience, even if they failed. The reason we concentrated on these people is because they are already convinced that home-based businesses work, even if their past experience with a particular company was not a success. Many of them already had the basic tools, such as a fax machine, or an office and desk to work at, or conference calling and call waiting. They already had contacts from their previous business experience, so that they could start setting appointments immediately.

The number one activity after prospecting must be cold calling. I believe that cold calling was more responsible for the explosive growth of our business than any other single thing we did or ever will do. No one ever called us and offered to become a partner. We had to get on the phone, consistently, and reach out to find people to become our partners.

Russ: Okay, Greg, suppose I'm in a networking business now, making a thousand dollars a month. I've been in it for a year. What would you say to me when I pick up the phone, if you have no idea who I am?

Greg: I have to establish a relationship. I have to understand who you are. It doesn't always work neatly. People will rarely spill the beans and tell you everything you need to know the first time you get in touch with them. We establish some kind of a relationship and dialogue with a person and build on that. Sometimes the relationship-building can begin on the spot, in the first call. Sometimes you have to follow up and make two or three calls before that person is finally going to give you the information you need to turn the conversation around and get the person to agree to meet.

I start by finding out where you're at with your business. I want to know how long you've been in the business. But, like I said, not everybody is willing to give me that information during the first interview.

I want to know how long you've been in your business, how many customers you have, how many of them have ordered, and what your income is. With those four standards, I can tell what may be important to you. I can tell you that for the same effort, in the same amount of time, with the same number of people, this is how much more success you could be experiencing in *our* business.

I want to know who your upline is and what kind of support you've been getting. One of the easiest people for me to be able to work with is somebody whose upline is in another state or very far away.

Russ: So, basically, you try to gather information that tells you the weakness or vulnerability of the contact's business. Then you exploit that knowledge by contrasting the strengths of your program with the weaknesses of your contact's program to motivate that person to take a look at the business you're offering.

Greg: In softer terms than that, Russ. But basically, yes. I need to learn *from them* the information I'm going to use to get them involved in my business.

Russ: What other activities do you do?

Greg: After prospecting and cold calling, the most important thing is *following up*. Going back to people who originally said "no" to us, or weren't sure, has proven to be one of the most lucrative skills we've mastered.

People don't call us back and say, "Okay, I want to work with you. I know you called me a couple of months ago and now I'm ready."

We had to be the ones who made the call. *We* had to initiate the follow-up.

We had to keep good notes, in some cases, *pages* of notes, detailing the highlights of our previous conservation so we could remember what was said the first time when we had a subsequent conversation with these folks. You'll be *amazed* by how favorably people responded to us when we remembered the details of our last conversation–for example, the best times to reach them or the names of a contact's spouse and children. We refer back to that to let them know that we took an interest in them and cared about what we talked about last time; that we were interested enough to remember the vacations they had been planning or the special

180

events in their lives they were looking forward to in our last conversation.

One of our most crucial tasks is to follow up with written material reaffirming the information we gave in our phone call. We know people will not remember the details of our phone call three months later. *These are activities we do on a daily basis.*

Sheri: This leads to making appointments to meet with the prospects. That's the only way we know to get our prospects on board so our income and theirs can grow. *Those are the only two things that we know will actually help our income grow.*

Too many people spend too much time on busy work which never grows their business. We don't spend a lot of time on that. We don't spend time with dreamers. We work with doers. We work with people who are coachable, consistent, self-motivated and product-centered. That's what we love to teach people. These skills help them to make appointments and keep their businesses profitable.

Russ: We've covered cold calling, following up, taking good notes, making appointments, doing the appointments, getting people into the business and teaching them to treat it like a business by becoming product-centered and staying focused. Are there other tips you could give, things you'll do today, and you'll do tomorrow, to grow your business?

Greg: One of the things I think is invaluable, and I know it sounds simplistic, is to read the magazines, periodicals, and other materials to learn about your industry, learn about your company and know where your company is headed, become familiar with the management team and understand and support the company's principles.

Find out who *leads* your company. Learn about the patents on the products. Learn about the industry and the growth and the growth rate and potential of the markets you are selling to. Find out what makes other people successful. We've learned *so much*

181

from other people! Others are learning a lot from us. We find that reading the magazines, keeping on top of current information, listening to the tapes, going over things that maybe we haven't looked at or reviewed in the last year or two helps us renew our thoughts and helps us rekindle ideas we haven't had in a while.

Interview #2:

Russ: Tom Barbieri is from Long Island. Working in my organization for the last few years, he's built a successful business of about a thousand customers.

I asked Tom, "What types of people do you recruit into your business? Why? What kind of people do you feel are good candidates to excel? What's their typical age and professional background? Why do you think these types of people excel? How do you go about trying to find these types of people and bring them into your business?"

Tom: I look for people who are *self-motivated*; people who are *success*-motivated. I don't think gender matters, or that there is any particular professional background or experience that is more successful in producing successful people. I talk with many people every day, and bring them through the recruitment process. I understand that *recruitment is not an event, it is a process*. You're looking for qualities like good time-management skills, and the ability–and the *willingness*–to be coachable.

It's very important, as you drive people through this business, that you allow them to settle where they want to be. I run with the runners. I walk with the walkers. I've worked with people from the construction industry, doctors and nurses, and computer technicians. The people who are successful in our business come from every walk of life.

The people I'm really looking for are those who have a burning desire to be more successful than they are today; people who are willing to put in the time and effort to make what they *want* to have happen *actually happen*; to become reality. They need really good time-management skills. Most important, I'm looking for people who are coachable; people who are willing to listen to what the leaders have to say about how they built their business, and are willing to follow them.

Russ: So you *look* for anybody and everybody. You give *everybody a chance* to hear about your business, but you *work with* people who have a burning desire to do the business, are coachable, and are willing to listen to the success methods that you offer to them.

Tom: Exactly. I'm looking for people who want to listen to what I have to say. I'm going to match their efforts. I'm not going to do more than they're going to do. I'm going to help them reach their goals. Like I said before, I really don't know whether there is a particular type of person who is more likely to succeed. We have college students, we have professional speakers, we have real estate owners, and we have people from every walk of life in this company. Don't pigeonhole yourself in the marketplace. Go out there and share your business with everybody. Work with those who are willing to work with you on a day-to-day basis. Team up, mentor them, and celebrate their success.

Interview #3:

Russ: Over the last three years, John and Beth McAdory have achieved explosive business growth in the Maryland area. They started their business part-time, and made it grow rapidly to an organization of over one thousand consumers. They saw their income go to several thousand dollars a month. With my mentoring, they're now aiming toward high achievement and status in their networking career.

I asked them to talk about a topic that was *crucial* to building their business, and is equally crucial to building *your* business.

183

"John and Beth, what business-building tools do you feel are essential to have when you are starting out in a networking business?"

Beth: In addition to product and marketing plan knowledge, we also look for business tools. Our company provides portfolios which give you all the business and product applications. Having those on hand for your customers and your business builders is a must.

As you get started in the business, you obviously need a fax machine and e-mail. You need to be able to get in touch with your business builders on an ongoing basis, so you're not always trying to catch up with them or having to leave messages on their phone.

Three-way-calling is one of our most important tools.

Russ: How do you use three-way calling?

Beth: In a variety of ways. When we have a new person on board, we make three-way calls with them when the newcomer contacts a prospect. New people have prospect lists of people they want to contact. Using three-way calling we're on the line with our new recruits each time they make a call to people on their lists. That allows us to train them on the phone. We hear what they're saying and can give them feedback and help them tweak it a little bit. It allows us to interact with our new people, bring them on board, get those appointments for them, and get them trained.

When we enroll a customer, we three-way call the company and introduce that person to the company. We walk the person through placing their order.

Three-way calling is a great way to give training. You, John, and I have done three-way calling with business builders, training them that way too.

Those are the kinds of the tools we use all the time. We also use books on marketing, how to keep your customers happy, and how to deal with people. If you are not continually feeding yourself, you are not growing as easily and as fast as you should.

184

Russ: Okay, so far your home office has business-builder kits to give to new people as they enroll with you, and three-way calling to help new people get trained and also to welcome them into the company and to help them make calls. You have e-mail capability and a way to keep in touch with your customers. Obviously you have an answering machine with a professional message.

Beth: We have a 10-year-old, but she has her own line. She doesn't answer our phone.

Russ: Looking around your office, is there anything else you have or you hand out, like calendars to keep people informed?

Beth: Absolutely. We have a hotline that people can call twenty-four hours a day, seven days a week, to learn what's coming up. We distribute calendars every time we have a meeting. We order brochures on new products from the company.

Russ: Do you have a formalized training packet that you give to new customers and new business builders?

Beth: Absolutely.

Russ: How many pages is it?

Beth: It starts out about five pages long.

Russ: Okay.

Beth: And we have our fast tracks.

Russ: What's a fast track?

John: That's an organized series of trainings. We cover specific topics: approaches, presentations, quality enrollments, closings, and the techniques that help you advance in the business. That's something our customers as well as our business builders can plug into if they have an interest in the business.

Russ: What is the timetable for these trainings?

Beth: Once a week for five weeks.

Russ: How long per session?

Beth: About an hour and a half.

Russ: Okay.

Beth: A half-hour of each session is set aside for participants to make phone calls and set up appointments. That helps us plan our week.

Russ: Do you feel this keeps your people accountable to their own goals?

Beth: *It keeps them in touch with their goals.* They are working on achieving them every day; they know what they're doing; they work through it from there.

Russ: It sounds like a lot of the tools you have are to keep in touch with the people in your organization, since this is a people business.

John: I think the biggest tool that we have in this business is the support we give our people. Being able to give energy and direction to the people we're working with is, without a doubt, the key. We have to be accountable to them. We have to know their commitment. We have to know what kind of time commitment they are going for, so we can commit to that for them, also.

Interview #4:

Russ: Jim McCune and his wife, Mary Martha McCune, live in West Virginia and Florida. They've built one of the most successful network marketing businesses in a company they've been with for over five years. They've had years of experience with other networking companies.

I asked Jim to talk about the skills that make him successful in networking, and to tell you how he learned them.

Jim: I've been in this business for five years and eight months. I'd been involved in other companies for about eleven years before that. I learned some basic things that have helped me along the way. First of all, *I am really big on my attitude*. I spend more time working on *myself* than I do on other people. I listen to tapes daily. I read daily. I encourage people to do that, because I know they have to grow, personally, and the books and tapes help speed their growth.

I've always built my business on the attitude that belief and commitment are the building blocks of my business. I believe people have to constantly work on their attitude, as I do, by reading and listening to tapes, by being around successful people, and by staying in touch with people, either personally or in conference calls, who have a *success attitude*. I believe in reading the basic books: *Think and Grow Rich, The Magic of Believing*, and *The Magic of Thinking Big*. I've read all those books–*several times*. I have a copy of *How to Win Friends and Influence People* that's almost worn out–*it is that basic and that important!*

I constantly work on my own attitude.

The second thing I developed very early was *belief*. I believe that there are *four beliefs* you have to have.

First, you have to *believe* in the product you are handling. You have to *believe* that everybody needs to be *at least* a customer–at the very minimum. That's what I've always believed about the company I'm involved with.

187

Second, you have to *believe* in the compensation plan offered by the company. *It makes a major difference.* You have to believe in it, because when you look someone in the eye, they have to know that *you* believe what you are saying.

Third, of course, is *belief in yourself.* Each action you take, *daily,* builds on that belief in yourself. It gives you more confidence. It gives you more belief in yourself and your ability to do what you are trying to do.

Fourth is *belief in other people.* I look at it like this: The first thing I do is attempt to see the good in other people. That attitude and outlook allows me to prospect them. That attitude allows me to talk to those folks who are good potential partners in my business.

The second part of my belief in other people is the Golden Rule: Treat other people as you would like to be treated. I'm friends with all kinds of people, all over the country, because I respect what they've done and they respect what I've done. I treat them the way I would like to be treated.

The third part of my belief in other people is believing that *they can do it.* People will do more because you believe in them than they will do on their own. You have to *believe* that everyone you talk to can make it. You have to *expect* them all to make it, but *you cannot count on **any one person** making it.* If you count on any one person making it, you will become disappointed and discouraged if they don't do so. *You can't let that happen!* If you do, you're setting yourself up for failure. I've learned to *never* let what anyone else says, thinks, or does disappoint or discourage me. If I do, that person is in control of my goals and my life–and *I won't let that happen!*

The fourth part of my belief system is that I don't complain about, condemn, or criticize the people I have in my business. If I do, that negative attitude transfers to them when I come in contact with them.

I built my business on *three basic principles:*

First, *consistency.* I am tenacious. I walk and talk my business. I've done that for five years and eight months. I do something to enhance my business *every day*. My goal is to meet a new person every day–someone to whom I can offer the opportunity to become involved, who I can bring into my business or show the business to.

I believe people have to actually schedule for themselves whatever time they've decided to commit to the business–but they *have to* schedule it! If they don't set a schedule and keep to it, they won't become business builders. They have to work their business like I work mine to be really successful. They have to work at it as they would work at a job–they have to show up for work every day. You have to show up for work in this opportunity, and consistently bring at least one or two new people a week into the business. If you do that yourself, you set the example. That's what leadership means. I believe the only way you can become a leader in any business is to take responsibility for setting an example. You never will be *appointed* a leader. If you are, it's not long-term. You have to *make* yourself a leader.

The second principle is *duplication*. I have developed my own training system. It's a duplicatable system. I know that if I can teach other people how to teach others, then I have truly duplicated myself. I use one basic approach with people. I tell them that I have something that works. I teach that constantly to people. I do the same presentation for everyone.

I listen only to those who have done what I want to do. I listen to nobody who has not done what I want to do. I never listen to new ideas just because they sound good. *Principles don't change.* If something isn't proven, I will not try it in my organization. You can't run an organization by trying new things just because some new guy comes into town and talks about it.

The third principle *is the sense of urgency*. I developed a sense of urgency from day one when I decided to do this business. I know the things I do today will determine what I will have for a long period of time after my retirement.

Always remember that most people do not *have to* do home-based businesses–but for those who choose to, and do it with a sense of urgency, their vocation will be their vacation. In other words, they'll be able to do whatever they want to do, when and how they want to do it.

I believe that if you build on these three principles of *consistency, duplication, and sense of urgency*, you will *only have to build one time*. It is easier to go fast than it is to go slowly in any kind of a home-based business because you have momentum going for you. The other people in your organization will pick up on it and develop their own belief systems for the four beliefs I've described.

Always remember, *leaders aren't appointed*. They *make* themselves leaders! You learn to lead by setting examples. People will do what you do—it's as simple as that. That's why I always stay out in front. I always enroll more people. I always contact more people. I always set the example for my people. I'm always tenacious about the business.

That's why I'm where I am.

Interview #5:

Russ: Raymond Aaron lives in Toronto. He's a very successful businessman and has a 3,500-person customer base in a networking company. He's going to talk about his background outside network marketing. I asked him why he feels network marketing is a great business for business people to get involved with, and what advantages network marketing offers, compared with other businesses he's been involved with.

Raymond: When I joined network marketing, I owned, and still own, a book-of-the month club and a monthly business coaching service. I teach an extremely successful course. I buy real estate for my own account. I'm a syndicator of real estate. I'm producing two *Chicken Soup for the Soul*-type books. I'm very busy giving lectures around North America.

I'm one of those rare creatures who was extraordinarily successful in business, who earned high income *before* joining network marketing. Many people get into network marketing as their hope for the way to make it, their hope for the way to pay the extra bills and get over the top and make their ends meet.

Once I joined, I realized that there were many benefits.

The first benefit of the network marketing company I've chosen is that there are no salesmen or distributors–there are only buyers. It may seem like an irrelevant point, *but it is a giant point*! In the network marketing company I'm involved with, each individual customer agrees to make a purchase each month, *on their own*, by placing an 800-call to the factory. They've agreed to do so, *in advance*, every month.

The giant relief, the giant silence, the giant calmness in my life comes from having thousands of people in my organization calling in their orders each month, on their own. That means my life is free of the running I had to do before. I don't call my customers every month to try to sell them. I don't send them letters or market them, or have a telemarketer contact them every month to try to make sales. I don't race around to their homes. They've agreed to buy *in advance*. That is a huge benefit to me.

The second benefit is relief from fluctuations in orders and income, relief from seasonality, and relief from lumpiness of income. "Lumpy" income is irregular cash flow. Money comes in a little bit now, a lot next month, nothing for a month or two, then more income, then less–the *total annual* income may be high, but any given month or period of several months–or sometimes even *years*–may produce little or no income. I know many high-income people. No matter how high their income may be, it's lumpy. I've seen that even some very high-income Realtors, for one example of people who live on commissions, have very bad credit ratings. They may go for two or three months getting almost no commission checks. During that time, their credit cards go overdue. As a consequence, although they easily earn enough money to pay their bills, and indeed by the end of the year have paid all their bills, there are unfortunate months where the income doesn't appear. If you're in a business with lumpy income, you can't count on the cash until you get the check.

In the network marketing company where I've been successful, lumpiness has been eliminated. Although I'm still involved in my other businesses–and the income from them is *still* lumpy–the network marketing company I've chosen has eliminated the financial valleys of the lumpiness by filling them in with a regular, smooth, predictable, and reliable income–a check I get on the same day of every month. No matter how high my income was, is, and will be, one of the greatest joys and reliefs of my life is the beauty of having no valleys, and having the valleys filled in by the regularity of my network marketing income, because everyone has agreed to buy each month.

The third benefit of network marketing is that there is no inventory and none of the overhead of typical businesses. When you look at a typical business, you look at tens of thousands of dollars being spent on office space, employees, attorneys, accountants, corporate taxes, corporation setups, and filing fees. In a typical business, you have employees, *whom you need to pay whether or not your business is profitable.* Then you have to worry about their pensions. In network marketing, you don't have any of this. These are a few of the huge benefits of getting involved with the network marketing industry.

Interview #6:

Russ: Steven Stam has built an organization of about 1,500 customers in the Long Island area. He works full-time for the city of New York as the head of the MIS department and does his networking business part time.

I asked him, "What mistakes did you make in building your business in the early stages of creating your organization that you would advise people *to avoid* as they start their businesses in network marketing?"

Steven: Russ, when I started in the industry, ten years ago, I made every mistake *possible!*

The first mistake I made is what I call the 'vomit factor.' As soon as I got home, I called a couple of my friends–you know, some real marketing types–and I vomited all the information I could remember right into their ears. I remember my friend Jim asking a few questions then telling me that it was all right, not to worry, and he'd visit me in jail regularly. I lost Jim forever because I vomited too much information on him. The bottom line was that I didn't know how to invite.

The second mistake I committed when I started my business was that I made my list too short. I had only about ten people I knew who I thought would be great at the business. I recommend, if you want to be serious about your business, that you be sure you have *at least 200 people on your list!*

My third mistake was to think that network marketing is just about money, not about products. You can't speak about your business with integrity if you don't know the products. Your prospects can see right through that. It's absolutely crucial to be thoroughly familiar with all the products! Get your hands on all the product samples you can. Test drive them for a couple of months. That will help you avoid thinking and talking just about money and keep you focused on the benefits of the products and services.

My fourth mistake was to try to mass-market instead of relationship-market. I expected to achieve massive growth by placing ads in the paper, putting up flyers, and doing penny-saver advertisements. I spent a lot of money trying to convince skeptical strangers to join with me. I didn't get much bang for my buck, because my paycheck and skill level were still low.

My fifth mistake was waiting for the great opportunity meeting. I used to wait for the once-a-month meeting to bring my new people to, rather than learning how to do a one-on-one presentation and small-group meetings throughout the month. I waited for that one bigwig to come into town to do a big meeting, thinking that if I brought new and potential customers and business builders to that meeting, that was all I had to do.

My sixth mistake was that I didn't treat this business seriously. I didn't create any urgency to get started with the business.

Because I didn't create urgency, my business grew slowly. This business is a little bit like NASA's space program. It takes a lot of energy to get your spaceship into orbit, but once it's in that orbit, it takes very little energy to keep it there.

The seventh and last big mistake I committed in the beginning was that I started out being pretty conceited. I thought that I knew everything and nobody could teach me anything. *I was not coachable.* At this point, knowing the business, I believe the best thing to be is coachable. Leave your ego at the door. Now that I'm successful, I know how to look for coachable people.

I strongly recommend that you respect the unique ways of networking and its powerful referral marketing approach, and avoid these seven mistakes of network "newbies," *regardless of how long you have been in any type of business before.*

Interview #7:

Russ: Steve Gordon and Laine Julian have had over ten years of experience in network marketing on a part-time basis. They've built organizations of a thousand or more people in two different businesses over the past ten years. They are very successful in my organization. We've been able to team up. They earn several thousand dollars a month, part-time. They're moving toward a very successful six-figure income in the business.

I asked them a very specific question so you might be able to avoid some of the pitfalls others have experienced in your business: "What are the three reasons why people fail in network marketing?"

Steve: The first and most important reason people fail, in our opinion, is that *they are not persistent and consistent. The only difference between the top money makers and the average earners in any program is that the top people have done more presentations.* We've seen people get to certain levels and then shift into a management mode. It is so important that, month after

194

month and year after year, people keep doing what they did when they first got started in the business.

Steve: The second reason for failure is *not being coachable*. The beauty of networking is that you have a built-in support and mentoring system. New people need to embrace their upline and their company training cycle. People need to become product-centered. When people realize a value and a benefit for a product line, they will order forever. That's what ensures a stable, long-term business. Finally, new members *must* team up and let their upline leaders do their first few presentations with them. This two-on-one system not only ensures that the new member has immediate success but also that he or she learns how to properly present the opportunity and handle objections.

Laine: The third reason for failure is *not treating their business like a business*. Because network marketing often starts out part-time, people tend to treat it as a hobby. A big business can be built *part time*, but not in your *spare time*.

Interview #8:

Russ: Dave and Lou Ann Cobb have had ten years of experience in network marketing and have built organizations of thousands of customers all around the world.

I asked them, "What do you feel successful leaders do that makes them succeed in the network marketing industry?"

Dave: In nearly ten years of network marketing we've discovered that everyone travels a unique path to success. Careful observation discloses a number of common denominators among successful people. We feel five concepts are very important.

First, successful leaders realize that the pace they set is the example for the rest of the organization. One of their primary goals is to advance to the first leadership level as soon as possible. Real leaders often advance one, two, or even three times in their first thirty to sixty days of involvement. Remember, you have *only one first month* in your business. Nearly every company has a position in the compensation plan that is generally deemed to be the threshold of real leadership. Get there as soon as you can. Your position in the marketing plan is a major indicator of your success.

Second, we all want lots of loyal customers who love our products and services–but *customers do not grow our business, business builders do*. While customers appreciate your products, business builders are looking for a check. If you want to attract other leaders, it's imperative that you create a respectable check *for yourself* as soon as possible.

Successful leaders utilize *every avenue in the compensation plan* to generate money. *They never leave any money on the table.*

Often, just a little extra effort can double your income. If you're generating a monthly check of hundreds or thousands of dollars, that will catch most people's attention. But when your monthly check goes over $10,000, you're really in the game.

There is no doubt about it, money talks!

Therefore, know your compensation plan inside and out and grow your check as fast as you can.

Third, great leaders are constantly recruiting new prospects and perfecting their presentation. These two components are crucial to success. Consistency and persistence in searching for new customers and leaders are the most vital aspects of growing your business. If you stop recruiting, your business will flatten. Recruit consistently and your business will explode.

Successful leaders work hard at developing a simple, straightforward presentation that's both compelling and duplicatable. This requires practice and persistence. Your presentation doesn't have to be eloquent, but it *must create urgency*. We have never seen a truly successful network marketer who can't move people to action. Great network marketers are like great athletes. They perfect the basics and consistently and persistently apply them.

196

Lou Ann: Fourth is a concept we call exposure. We've seldom seen a successful network marketer who hasn't created positive exposure for himself. In other words, you need to be visible, to be seen as a leader. Real leaders don't sit quietly at the back of the room. Instead, they hunger to be in the front of the audience telling their stories. They take advantage of every opportunity to do so. When contests, awards and recognition are available, they go all-out to win. These tools are designed by your company to provide the outward evidence of your success.

Your advancements and accomplishments, your pictures and articles in the company magazines, and your participation at the elite levels of the company all build your credibility and exposure as a leader. Successful leaders look the part and act the part.

Last, we want to emphasize the importance of *team building*. Everyone who has succeeded knows you don't make it on your own. You never see great leaders all by themselves. On the contrary, they're always clustered together. Successful leaders have learned the value of teaming up for appointments, presentations and trainings.

Building strong relationships by working together is fundamental to success.

Your *residual income* will be a function of your *residual relationships*. *If you want the income, build the relationships.* When you're as genuinely interested in someone else's success as in your own, you've learned the real secret of greatness in this industry.

Over the last four years, we've had the great good fortune of teaming up with Russ Paley, learning his success methods and duplicating them throughout our organization. This has led us to be very successful network marketers with a full-time income of over six figures each and every year.

Interview #9:

Russ: Bill Lang is an attorney in the New Jersey area. He's also a very successful marketing executive whom I've trained and mentored over the last few years. I asked him, "When a confirmed appointment doesn't show up for the scheduled meeting, what do you do?"

Bill: I call the person and try to find out why he or she didn't show up. Then I use the no-show's time by making more telephone calls to set new appointments. I've set aside that time anyway, so I shift to a different aspect of the business; making more appointments.

It's important to understand that, even when you've done everything possible to confirm an appointment, there will be some no-shows. Don't be discouraged or disappointed no matter how wonderful you think the individual might have been for the business. A no-show most likely would be a thorn in your side. The simple fact that the prospect was a no-show is a sure sign, in almost all cases, that the prospect is not reliable. Extenuating circumstances do exist–say a trip to the hospital emergency room–but they're rare.

I've found that if I confirm an appointment twice, it greatly reduces the no-show possibility. I've also found that if I go to them–if I go to the prospects offices, or to their homes, rather than asking them to come to me–it decreases the likelihood that they are not going to show up.

The other thing I do, when I confirm appointments, is to sound excited and convey a lot of enthusiasm. When I call back after they fail to show up for the meeting, I sound excited, like they really missed something. When I reschedule the appointment with them, they will probably show up.

Interview #10:

Russ: Marlin Hershey introduced me to network marketing, about eight years ago. We've worked together in two businesses. I asked him, "What challenges have you encountered in your business over the years you've been in the industry? How have you overcome them?

Marlin: The biggest challenges for most people, including myself, have been the *mental challenges*.

Mental challenges are things that happen between your right ear and your left ear. They're quite different from the other challenges you face when you start in the business, like learning how to invite, and giving a good presentation. The mental challenges are when you ask yourself, over and over, *Is this real? Can I be successful? Will my goals and dreams and passion for succeeding last? Will it really happen?*

This is a business where you're building a residual income. You *are not* making a salary. This makes it so different from what most people are used to that they find themselves facing the mental challenge of looking at their work and income in a whole new and different way.

Another mental challenge for many people is having to ask for other peoples' approval. In doing that, whether it means they tell people what they are doing or try to show people the opportunity they're involved with, they constantly get peoples' opinions–and often those opinions are negative. You don't find a lawyer, a doctor, or a school teacher out there every day trying to tell people what they do and inviting them into their industry. We set ourselves up for a lot of punches most people don't ask for, expect, or take in their "normal" lives. When they're hit by such a punch, they often don't take it well. I overcame that by knowing in my heart why I'm doing this. I have a deep belief in the system and in myself, in my company and its products–and *absolutely*, I have a goal.

The other major mental challenge you face is that you deal with people. The best part about people is dealing with them–and the worst part about people is dealing with them!

Russ, when we first worked together, you set an incredible pace. You had an incredible vision. You knew what you wanted to achieve, and you pretty much knew what I wanted to achieve. You often involved yourself with a lot of people who were part time, and this business was the second, third, fourth, or fifth thing on their importance list–which is pretty true for most of us. But you kept your focus on what you wanted to achieve, and most of all you worked with those who wanted to achieve success, *now.*

The last challenge is that people in this business will run hot and cold. They will build their businesses to a certain level, whether that's the level they really want, or they just find a comfort zone at a certain income and effort level where they no longer want to go out and do the things that they need to do to create success and continue to increase their income. As uncomfortable as people often are when they first get into this industry, their comfort level is just as far to the other side after they achieve a certain degree of success.

You always have to keep yourself aligned with your goals. Always work to make your passion for this business greater than it is today.

Russ, I think that ultimately we have a responsibility, as we achieve our goals, to help other people achieve theirs. As leaders, we have to remember that where they are now is where we were two years ago, four years ago, ten years ago.

I think if each person we bring into our organizations can overcome the mental challenges by staying on-track and having a goal, and if they can learn to really deal with people, they will achieve success.

Interview 11:

Russ: Andrew Coppola is an executive I trained. He has developed an organization of over fifteen hundred customers in two years. He was one of the top ten highest producers in our marketing company in 1998. I asked him, "What do you do to recognize the achievements of people who are advancing in the marketing program?

Andrew: Recognition is an ongoing process. When my people advance to the first leadership level, I personally congratulate each of them on the phone and help them understand that this is just the beginning. I help them see the power behind residual income–that they are getting a check every month, even if they do not continue building their businesses and just remain customers.

I have my new business builder speak with others in the organization to get a feel from their stories and learn how long it took them to achieve their levels. I celebrate their successes by having those who have advanced to a new level meet the top income earners. I give them front seats at trainings. My theory is that if a new business builder can see a part of the lifestyle of other successful business builders who have just advanced, the newcomer will be inspired to focus on his or her goals, see the lifestyle that networking makes possible, and strive for further advancement.

Reaching the next big step in the compensation plan is an occasion of major significance. I make sure we really celebrate each person's achievement, with a special dinner with all the leaders on their team. This is their night, and they deserve it. A nice gift is presented at this dinner to further appreciate and honor the business builder's advancement to the middle levels of the compensation program.

I continually celebrate success as people advance in my business. People want to know they are appreciated. Sending cards and leaving messages on their answering machines are great ways to thank them.

I make sure successful leaders contact people who have achieved new advancement in their business. That contact and support is one of the keys to my continued success.

Interview #12:

Russ: Joe Mirrione is a 1998 college graduate who has built a business of three hundred customers while getting a Pharmacy degree. I asked him, "What do you do when someone you present to doesn't want to sign up?" This is a key point, because many beginning networkers don't know what to do or say at that point.

Joe: I ask them whether they would be willing to help by referring me to others who are entrpreneurial and might be interested in enhancing their lives. When I get a name from them, I ask for another, and another, until they run out of referrals. If I feel that the prospect is really *right* for the business and has potential to be successful with me but the timing isn't right for them, I ask whether I may have their permission to keep in touch with them to keep them updated on my progress in the business. Then I send them postcards from each of the half-dozen vacation spots I visit each year. You'd be amazed how many people actually thank you for the postcards when you call them to follow up!

Interview #13:

Russ: Ronald Dent is a top executive in his business. He's built a strong business, mainly in the New York area, of over fifteen hundred customers.

I asked him, "What do you do when someone first enrolls into the business and wants to be just be a customer?"

Ronald: My wife and I know that eighty to ninety percent of everyone coming into the business will be *only a customer* and *will not build the business.* We put extra emphasis on this aspect of our success. Our goal is to teach people to shop through our store. When we do our presentation, a large amount of time is spent *strictly on the products.* We know that even if they never build a business, if we keep them as customers we will have them forever. We use a product comparison sheet so that they know that whatever they now spend on products we retail, they will get better products for less from our company.

Once we use the product cost comparison sheet against their current expenditures for comparable products they use in their home, they realize how much more economical it would be to become customers. They see that they can sometimes go six to eight months without needing to replace the same product, and that there are plenty more products they need that they can buy. This is a very effective way to avert the argument that the monthly minimum purchase requirement exceeds their normal consumption and their budget. They can see that they'll have no problem purchasing enough products to remain on customer status with the company.

Last, we call the new customer a week after their first order was placed to confirm that they are satisfied with the products. We mail them a reminder postcard in their second month with us, to assure that they won't forget to order.

Interview #14:

Russ: Bryan Lazaroff and his wife have built a business of over two thousand customers. They were in the top ten in 1998, based on their fast growth, in the networking company they represent.

I asked, "Bryan, how long is your initial presentation to a prospective new customer or business builder? What do you cover within a presentation to make it effective and to get that person interested in joining?"

Bryan: When I sit down with an individual or group, my initial presentation is approximately forty-five minutes to an hour long. To stay within my allotted time, I arrange for a quiet location and pay strict attention to time. Keep in mind that this is a business meeting. Adults and children have very similar attention spans. Have you ever noticed the length of time for one class period in school? It's approximately forty-five minutes to one hour. *Any presentation longer than one hour will decrease your chance to close.*

I cover five main topics in my presentation. This format, I believe, will build up to a very simple close.

1: I start with my story. (Approximately five minutes.) This includes how I was introduced to the company. I also explain my previous business background. This is essential to break the ice.

2: The company's story (approximately ten minutes), with the mission statement, the goals of the company, and its track record. Many people you sit down with will want to know the company information for a sense of security.

3: The products and services. (Approximately fifteen minutes.) This is the meat of my presentation. Although this represents the bulk of the information, the time allotted for this topic should be kept to *no more than fifteen minutes*. *Giving too much information can be poisonous.* I like to ask questions during this part to get feedback. By this time your prospective customer is warming up to you.

4: The compensation plan. (Approximately ten minutes.) Focus on the money. The majority of the people in attendance are there to find out how they can earn additional income. The products and/or services are always the driving force, but most people say "show me the money." Therefore I motivate, instill confidence, and express the win-win philosophy: *we all get paid together.*

5: Last, *but not least*, is the close. (Approximately five minutes.) *This is the most important step.* By this time I can sense whether my audience has questions, whether my audience is one person or a room full of people. (It's rare that they have no

204

questions–and if they don't, it may mean that they're bored or not interested.) I answer the questions and begin my close. Please understand that *if you have a **weak close**, you will lose **every time!*** Never ask a yes-or-no question. (It gives people a chance to say no.)

These are some examples of a strong close:

"Do you see yourself more as a customer, or as someone who wants to build residual income for life?"

"What did you like best about the program? Great, let me show you how to get started now!"

Be strong, confident, and, most of all, consistent

Interview #15:

Russ: Dan Tore is a top executive with a large networking company. He's built a business of over two thousand customers in four years. I asked him, "What do you do when someone first signs up and wants to do the business with you?"

Dan: The first thing I do is make sure the prospects understand that *they must be product-centered*. To become product-centered, I recommend that each person purchase a pack of products so that they can do a test drive with the company's products right away.

The next thing I do is distribute a getting-started packet of training information describing the steps which they must take. These steps include writing down their goals and creating their contact list, reading the information, and watching the videos and audios provided by the company.

Two days after these assignments are made, I book an appointment with them. I want to make sure they're committed to the business. I want to know that *before* I spend energy building their businesses with them. On the night before the follow-up, I call to make sure that the prospect has completed writing down the contact and goal lists, has read the training materials, and is ready for the follow-up. If the prospect is not ready, I reschedule the follow-up appointment so the person can do those assignments before we meet. (If they don't do the assignments, I know I have customer, not a business builder.)

At the follow-up, I *first* go over the person's goals. I want to see what drives the person and why he or she wants to do the business.

Second, I review the contact list and highlight the names the person has identified as the best prospects on his or her list.

Third, I review the person's planned store hours to determine when and how much time they can devote to building the business. That tells me whether the person's goals are realistic.

Fourth, I role-play with the new person, teaching the proper way to make calls and set appointments. I try to set some appointments, working with the new person, especially if they seem reluctant to get on the phone and make calls–which suggests they might not make the first call without my help. I do all I can to get them prepared and motivated.

Fifth, In follow-up meetings with my new people I get on the phone with them and have them make appointments.

When they experience rejection in a situation where I'm there with them, I can reassure them that this is part of the business and they shouldn't let it bother them. This *definitely* helps them understand how calling and inviting works. That experience and support from me goes a long way to making sure they have the inviting skills down so they're ready to set appointments on their own.

Sixth, the final thing I do is get the new person to go out and do appointments with me. I like to do five to ten appointments with each person so that, with my help, the person can see the presentation working and see people signing up right away.

Interview #16:

Russ: Roland Roberts is an executive with a network marketing company. I trained him and helped him build a business of over one thousand customers in the Brooklyn area.

I asked him, "What do you do when someone stops working the business and stops using the products?"

Roland: Whenever someone stops using the products or drops out of the business, I call to find out what caused him or her to make that decision.

Most times I find that the person was not enrolled properly, did not get any assistance in placing orders, or did not receive sufficient training.

Those who enjoy the products and get support are usually loyal and do not quit.

One of the most common reasons for people to stop doing the business or stop using the products is lack of knowledge about the business and the products. I try to correct that when I call them and get them refocused on the value of the products and the business.

Other factors which may contribute to people continuing with the business are the relationships I develop with them and the assistance I provide. I show them that we care about them and want to help them make money. When I build rapport and make this a people-related business rather than just a business of numbers, people feel we care about them. Hopefully, they will come back in and work the business and use our products again if they feel we absolutely believe they're on our team and we really do care about their success.

Interview #17:

Russ: Chris O'Neill has built a business of about six hundred customers in the New York area. She's very product-centered, which is why she has exceptionally high retention of her customers.

I asked her, "Why did you believe it was so important for you to become product-centered at the beginning, when you first got started in your business?"

Chris: First, if your new prospect asks a question about a product, you can answer it with confidence from first-hand experience.

Second, you will be able to give personal testimonials which are an integral part of your personal story. Personal testimonies, not technical product knowledge and ingredient information, are what sell the product or service. Everyone can duplicate their own personal stories, whereas many may not know much about the specific ingredients of products or the technical details of services.

Third, your efforts will make you a *product of the product*, and that attitude and practice will help others duplicate your attitude, practices, and success throughout your business. People will do what you do. That gets you from point A to point B faster, and helps you build a more solid and knowledgeable organization.

Fourth, instead of people in your organization just doing the minimum required to make money, they try products that they probably wouldn't have tried. This raises your volume in your organization. These additional items may be the very reason why a person decides to tell other individuals to get started with the business.

Fifth, quality, value and service are why customers shop at a company and stay. Your personal loyalty to the product and commitment to quality, value and service are crucial to assuring the growth of your business.

Sixth and last, the statistics prove that only ten percent of enrollees will do the business. The other ninety percent will be customers. If customers are using more products than the minimum, they will be customers forever. They may even do the business sometime down the road. This means you earn a larger residual income, on a larger customer base, for a longer period of time.

CHAPTER TEN

TEN PROVEN TIPS TO TAKE YOU TO THE TOP

I n this final chapter, I want to talk about the ten things every successful network marketer does, constantly, every day of every week, month and year. These are the things *you must do if you expect to be successful.*

I cannot stress *"must do"* too strongly. *These are the steps to success.* Skip or slight one, and you will fail–and I didn't write this book to tell you how to fail!

I've already covered the key points of building a successful networking business. I want to stress the *ten key activities and traits* shared by all great networkers.

First, all great leaders in our industry sign up a *minimum* of four new customers a month. New blood is truly the life blood of your business.

There are many reasons why it is *so critical* to continue to prospect and enroll new people into your network. Your *personal* activity, the work you do *personally* to sign up new people, *sets the pace for everyone in your organization.* Your people look to you as their leader.

Your activity and success creates new excitement in them as they see the growth of your business. They see that new customers are the fertilizer for a healthy year ahead, for you and for them. They–those who are business builders, not customers–will follow your example and do the same. You may inspire some who begin as customers to become business builders.

To make this fertilizer for business-growth super grade, a great networker assures that at least one of the four (or more) new customers he or she signs up will be a business-minded person–a business builder. To achieve this, the great business-building networkers recruit until they find at least one business builder each and every month. They find someone among their first four new recruits or keep recruiting until they find that one important person. Recruiting customers is certainly important, but recruiting business builders is what makes your organization grow. Adding business builders creates duplication, more growth, and more excitement than just signing up four customers to use your product or services.

If you recruit four new people each month, and at least one of the four is a business builder, at the end of each year you will have forty-eight new customers, of whom at least twelve will be building the business.

Networking is a numbers game, so you have to expect that a certain percentage will continue to build the business–but *some will stop* for any of the various reasons I've talked about. *That's why it's so critical to bring in new customers and builders each month.* If some of your people don't produce–and, count on it, some won't–at the end of each year you'll still have enough people duplicating your efforts to grow your business.

Second, all great leaders help one of the people they've signed up to advance to the first leadership level during each thirty to ninety-day period. If you just sign up people into your business you won't have a walk-away income. You *must* sign up people *continuously and consistently*, and develop a certain number of them into leaders of your business, if you expect to retire with an income that will support your retirement.

Identify one person in each one-to-three-month period on whom you can focus your energy. Work to develop that person until he or she achieves the first leadership level. That's the key to a profitable lifelong business. This person should do all the homework assignments I covered in Chapter Four. If he or she has problems with any assignment or any step in the process, be sure you're there to help the person get over whatever hump appears to be in the way of his or her success.

If you do this, you will have anywhere from four to as many as twelve new business builders *per year* making money and duplicating your efforts in your business. This is a good number to handle. If you're doing the business very part-time, develop one person every quarter. Full-time networkers should work with a new leader every month.

Third, a great networker is persistent and consistent. Persistence means that you do not listen to the dream stealers. Dream stealers may be friends and family who are either jealous or don't understand what you're doing. They're honestly scared that you may fail–so instead of supporting your quest for success, they try to get you to stop doing the business. You *must* stay focused on your long term goals, and believe entirely in the company you work with.

The best analogy I can give is driving a car. If you keep your eyes and attention on the road at all times, you will get to your destination much faster and more easily than if you keep looking off the road.

Continuing the analogy, when you drive your car consistently at a certain speed, you will get to your destination more quickly than if you constantly change speed.

A great leader needs to be consistent in building his or her business. Your new business builders are looking up to *you* for your leadership. If *you* are consistent, *they* will be, too. If *you* are inconsistent, *they* will be inconsistent.

In *any* industry, inconsistent business practices lead to problems and failure. Just imagine if your local supermarket was open some nights, and some weekends, but closed whenever the manager felt like it. When you shop, you count on the supermarket being open twenty-four hours a day, seven days a week–or always open for specific hours and days. Would you keep shopping there if you arrived and found it closed for no apparent reason, *once*? Especially if it happened *twice*? Not likely!

The consistency factor is absolutely just as important in your networking business!

I would rather work with someone who *consistently* works five hours a week to develop their business, than with someone who works forty hours a week *once every two months*, and *zero* hours a week every other week.

Fourth, great leaders are always positive, honest, and helpful to everyone growing the business. They *always* help others. When leaders have a bad day, or face challenges that seems insurmountable–and everyone has their share of those–they call their enrollers, successful, positive people in their upline, or call the company. They do not call people below them in their organization. It's the same principle your parents probably followed when you were young. If they were fighting, they'd try to resolve it between themselves without involving their children in the disagreement. In this analogy, the people in your downline are your "children." The people in your upline are the people you can look to for help in solving problems you can't handle alone, just as you looked to your parents for help when you were a child.

Integrity is an important quality most great leaders share. Integrity means *always* being honest with the people who look up to you, and always doing the right thing for your new person's business.

One example might be a new person's first order. It might make you money–right now–to talk the new person into placing a big order, to buy more than he or she really needs. That would make you more money right then, from that order. That's both unethical and short-sighted. In the long run you'll make far more money–and feel better about it–if you treat your new people as you would treat your own family members, giving them good advice and doing right by them if asked to advise what they should buy for their first order. If they buy what they need, and don't feel like their house is full of unused products you talked them into ordering, they're a

212

lot more likely to order again the next month, and the next. They'll order what they need and will use, and know they were treated honestly and with integrity. Your helping attitude and integrity will come back to boost the commitment level of your business builders.

Great leaders always match energy with energy, and will do any meeting, follow-up training, phone call, or other tasks needed or requested to support the people in their business who help others in their business grow and prosper. There is no one-way street to success in this industry. You must put other peoples' goals on the same level of importance as you place your own. To achieve success, *it's just as important for them to reach their goals and dreams* as it is for you. Networking is a team effort–very similar to a great sports franchise.

Fifth, great leaders have *specific goals–which they revise often.*

Short term goals are important since they are within your reach and you can plan daily activities to accomplish them. However, a great networker also has a tangible long-term goal. That long-term goal is the fuel for your engine. It will motivate your work ethic in building your business.

Short term goals are one month to six months in length. They are always time and goal specific.

How many new customers will you bring into your business *this month*?

How many new business builders will you bring into your business *this month*?

What status level will you hit *this month*?

What will your status be *six months from now*?

How many *hours a week* can you commit to the business in the *next six months*?

How much money will you make in the *next three months*?

213

Long-term goals are set for a year or more. They are necessarily less specific and more general, and can be subject to revision if you find that your progress is faster or slower than you anticipated. Revising goals to reflect reality is important. If you can revise goals upward, that's what this business is about. That's wonderful–and it's often an unstated but understood long-term goal. However, if you find you have to revise downward, take a look at your goals and determine why you need to make that change. Were you over-optimistic? Is there some step in the process you're having difficulty with? When you have to revise long-term goals downward, first ask yourself, "Why?" See whether you can identify the problem. Then talk to the people in your upline. They, after all, have been through everything you're going through, or they wouldn't be where they are.

Long-term goals are set like this:

How many customers do you want in your business in *three years*? How many do you want in *five years*?

What status do you want to reach *three years* from now? Where do you want to be *five years* from now?

Tangible goals are the visible signs of success. As you achieve each tangible goal, consider it a "trophy" of the achievements you want to make. Most companies also hand out physical trophies to those who succeed, and it's nice to have those trophies on your mantle or hanging on your wall, but the real trophy is your success; the achievement of the tangible and intangible goals you set.

In *three years*, once you have achieved your long term goal, *what do you want to do with the money?* Pay off your debt, get a new car, house, boat? In *five years*, what will you do with the *savings* you've built up from your customer base?

Sixth, all great networkers treat their businesses like *big* businesses. Though you can start with almost nothing, *it is indeed a big business*–but *you* have to work to make it so, and *you* have treat it like one.

214

I got started in this industry for about $350, which included all the products, literature, and sign-up information–but *from that day I always treated my business as if I had just invested a million dollars.* This helped me create urgency within myself to achieve success quickly. It affected how I talked about my business to others, and that helped me sign up business-builders early on, *before* I was making any substantial income.

I believe that if your mind-set is that you are involved in the biggest and best business of your life, and that it's your ticket to financial success in life–whatever that means to you–you have the ingredient found in all successful leaders in this industry.

Seventh, all great leaders celebrate success. Remember that most people are not often congratulated for a job well done in their work or personal lives–if at all. However, human nature dictates that people will do more if they know that other people care about and recognize their success. Recognizing another person's success is the key to motivation. (Just as recognizing your own success and feeling good about it motivates you.)

If you're good at letting people know that you've recognized their success and honor it, whether your recognition is a phone call, a post card, or other public or private recognition, you can expect your business builders to continue working hard.

I do everything from making personal calls to those in my business who advance to new levels every month, to sending holiday gifts, letters, and plaques, and hosting award dinners where I can let people know that I care about and recognize their efforts.

Eighth, never forget the basics that brought you to the level of success you have attained, and will take you to higher levels.

Every day, even seven years after my business started, I continue to prospect, do follow-up trainings, one-on-one meetings, group meetings, and sign up new people for myself. I believe all successful people repeat the basics that made them successful in the first place, over and over again, in order to continue their success and assure that it not only continues, but grows.

I'm sure that Michael Jordan, during his last season (1998, when his Chicago Bulls won the NBA championship again), continued to practice just as hard as he did in the 1970's when he was still in junior high school. He continued to practice shooting lay-ups and free throws, and all the other elements of his game that made him possibly the finest player who ever played professional basketball.

The basics become easier over time, and with repetition. More advanced methods of recruiting, like cold calling or using the Internet, can be added to the basics, once the basics are mastered–*and continued.*

Ninth, leaders set up an environment where they love the people they work with, love their schedules, and love helping others. I believe that to be *truly great* at something, *you must love what you do.*

Most great leaders in networking choose to work with people they get along with. They also make their schedule so that they truly enjoy doing the business.

I used to cold call for many hours in a row, but found I became unproductive after the third hour–*because I didn't enjoy it anymore.* Obviously, no business is enjoyable *all* the time, and sacrifices need to be made to achieve success, but leaders have an overall love for their business, and their future with that business. That's why they're so committed to it. Leaders know it's a team effort, and love helping others make money. They know that when they help others make money, they also make money.

Tenth, leaders set the pace in every aspect of their business. The speed of the leader is the speed of the crew.

Leaders do all the activities I've talked about in this book. They lead by example. They attend *every single function* that's important to their business.

216

I always attend every meeting, training, and convention. I buy every tape and training book I can get my hands on to continue to grow my knowledge and better my organization.

Leaders never stop learning and are always looking for better ways to build their business. They're always looking for ways to add to and refine the basic and advanced techniques that have worked for them in the past. The more your knowledge base grows, the more your business will grow into the 21st century.

APPENDIX A

TAX-SAVING TIPS FROM A CPA WHO HAS BEEN THERE

Russ: I'm at the home of Randy Fischel, a CPA in the Long Island area. I asked him to talk about some of the tax advantages of running your own home-based business. I also asked Randy to talk about how long he's been an accountant, how many clients he has, what types of home-based businesses his clients own, and the experience that qualifies him to talk about this topic.

Randy: I've been an accountant for about seventeen years. I've had my own practice for fourteen years. My practice currently has between one hundred fifty and two hundred personal tax returns, and sixty businesses. Over the years I've handled hundreds of businesses. Many of them have been home-based.

The home-based businesses I've handled have included construction companies, attorneys, and consultants.

All businesses have overhead, but overhead is different with a home-based business. I realized this when I took a good look at an accounting practice I shared with a partner. It had the overhead of employees, rent, and all the other expenses of a normal business. I looked at those expenses and saw that they were hurting the bottom line–tremendously. Many weeks, after paying the bills and the employees, there was not much left for my partner and myself. At that point I decided I was going to take my business back into my home.

When I ran the business from my home, most of those overhead expenses were no longer there. That created a larger bottom line. With a smaller practice, but working from my home, I earned more money. *That is what a home-based business is all about.*

A lot of my clients have home-based businesses. They chose to do it that way because they didn't want the risk, expenses and overhead of conventional businesses.

A typical business that keeps twenty-five percent of the gross, or even ten or twenty percent is fortunate, because overhead eats so much of the cash coming in.

One of the things about a home-based business, and one of the reasons why I looked at Russ's business and got involved with him, is because I looked at the tax returns of people doing home-based networking businesses and saw that their bottom line was sixty percent or more of the gross, *even as much as eighty percent of the gross*! That's *awesome*! That's what business is all about.

It is not how much you bring in. It is how much you keep.

That's why you see a typical business, say a restaurant that has great food, go out of business after a few months. You wonder why, thinking wow, they had great food! Why did they go out of business? There was just too much overhead. A home-based business eliminates the overhead. It's the way to go, today.

After examining and working with people who run home-based businesses, and especially with people like Russ and his partners, I found that the gross was six figures, *but the net was also six figures!* Most of the normal (non-home-based) businesses I handle might have a high-six-figure *gross*, but because of the high overhead, they *net* very little.

I handled a man who sold semi-precious stones. His business did over a million dollars a year, gross, but his bottom line net would be sixty to seventy thousand dollars. That's an okay income, but *as a percentage of gross that is not where I want to be.*

One benefit of a home-based business is that you can deduct normal expenses you've already incurred, and would incur anyway, like your house or car. If you have a home-based business, they become business expenses *to an extent*. *This is crucial to understanding the tax benefits of a home-based business.* You can deduct expenses *to the extent* of the percentage of those expenses that can be attributed to your business, according to IRS guidelines.

In other words, if you use your car fifty percent for business, you can't write off the whole car. You'd write off fifty percent.

There are different kinds of expenses in a home-based business. The two kinds of expenses I'm talking about are:

First, expenses you incur *only* because you are in that business. Most of these are fully deductible. Your tax professional will know the exceptions, and what percentage of them you can deduct.

Second, expenses you already have, and would have anyway, like your home, your telephone, and your car. The "business use" percentage of these expenses can be deducted.

The first kind of expenses are those you wouldn't have had if you weren't in the business. In most networking businesses, these expenses are usually minimal. There's the start up cost, the promotional fees, maybe the costs of traveling and fees to go to meetings, and an extra telephone line. You might buy a computer and fax machine for your business. You'd have business postage, and a lot of small incidental expenses–supplies and that sort of thing. Those are the smaller costs, but what I've seen in my experience is that most of the expenses of a home-based business are expenses that you already have. That's what really adds more money to your bottom line.

The first of those expenses would be your automobile. You probably already have a car. For tax purposes, we list the actual expenses of that car and add up the total. We figure what percentage of your total mileage was business mileage for that

220

home-based business. You write off that percentage of your car. To do so, you must keep a "contemporaneous record" (an IRS term) of the actual miles driven for business purposes, and what the business purpose was. That means that you keep a little milage and expense log book in the car and develop the habit of writing down the starting and ending mileage of each business trip. It's simple, once you get in the habit of keeping that record.

Let's say your car payment is four hundred dollars a month, on a lease for a car you would have had whether you were in business or not. Because you're in business and use the car in that business, you can now deduct half of that (if the car was used fifty percent for business). This is legitimate, because you are using that car for business. To figure the car expense, we would take the total of all the auto expenses, which would be the lease payment or the cost of the car, insurance, repairs, gas, bridge and highway tolls (if you live in an area with toll roads and bridges), parking expenses and things like that, and multiply that total by the percentage of your total milage that was for business purposes. The result is your deduction. Fifty percent business use equals a fifty percent deduction.

Your home office is the second major deduction. You're either paying rent or paying a mortgage, with mortgage interest, real estate taxes, water and sewer taxes, insurance, utilities, heat, repairs, landscaping, the exterminator–things like that. All those are expenses you would have had anyway.

Now, if you use part of your home *exclusively for your business*, (the IRS is fussy about what that means; check with your accountant or tax professional to be sure your home office complies) you can take the percentage of your home that you use for business and take it as a deduction. Let's say the expenses I just mentioned add up to two thousand dollars a month. If you use 250 sq. ft. of a 1,000 sq. ft. home for your business, you can now deduct $500 (twenty-five percent) of the expenses I listed. (If you

221

use 250 sq. ft. of a 4,000 sq. ft. home, the percentage is lower, of course.) Again, you would have had those expenses even if you weren't in the business, but now you can deduct them from your income. That puts more of your normal expenses on the bottom line for tax purposes.

If you have a separate business telephone, it's fully deductible. If you use the same phone for business that you do for your personal life, the business use portion of your telephone bill is deductible.

You might entertain or take people out to dinner. If you go out with a friend and pick up the tab, and during that meeting you talked about your home-based business, fifty percent of the dinner bill is deductible. You might have gone to dinner with that person even if you weren't in the business, but you have your business and discuss it with your friends. If your *intention* was to talk about the business when you went to that dinner, fifty percent of that meal and fifty percent of business-related entertainment expenses will be deductible.

As with your auto expenses, it is essential to keep a diary of these expenses, and to obtain receipts for everything possible, so you can prove your deductions when it comes time to prepare your return. That "contemporaneous record" (in IRS terms) is also a vital back-up in the event you're ever audited.

To summarize:

In a home-based business, your overhead is low.

Certain fixed expenses can be reduced because you will be able to deduct a portion of them from your gross business income.

Your net income, both as a percentage of gross income and in absolute dollars, will be much higher compared to a conventional business of equal gross.

Always check with your tax professional about what you can deduct (the rules change a little each year) and how he or she wants you to keep the records that support your deductions.

Then there is the residual income in businesses like the one I'm in, where you get paid for the rest of your life for something you do once.

To give you my own example, I started my other (non-accounting) home-based business in 1993. I've built it for those five and a half years *strictly* on a part-time basis. I do very little with it during some of January, all of February and March, and part of April. January 15 to April 15 is the heavy-duty tax-season part of my accounting business. I probably work seventy to eighty hours a week–or even more.

A funny thing happened last April. When I received my check for March, it was in excess of $16,500–*for a month in which I didn't even do any work on my networking business!*

223

I devoted very little time to the networking business last March, probably less than five hours for the entire month. I received a check for over $16,500 in a month during which I did hardly anything for that business! That's the reward you get from the residuality of a networking business.

"Reading Network Your Way to Millions will make you unstoppable in your network marketing business."

—CYNTHIA KERSEY, author of *Unstoppable*

"This great book is invaluable; a must read. Following Russ's plan can make anyone wealthy."

—THOM WINNINGER
Ex-president of National Speakers Association
Author of three books: *Sell Easy, Price Wars, Hiring Smart*

"Russ's inspirational book teaches the concept of compounding residual income. Read it and implement it, and your success will follow."

—MARLIN HERSHEY
Made $3 million in network marketing
Ultra-successful networker

"I strongly recommend Russ Paley's guide to success. His grasp of network marketing is astounding. The best revenge is massive success. Russ's teaching will help you get there."

—LEONARD HALL, Las Vegas, NV
An Amway Crown Direct
Author of numerous training manuals

"Russ owes his success to the systematic way he approaches business. You owe it to yourself to learn from the master."

—JOHN STEFANCHIK
Creator of *The Stefanchik Method*
Author of nine books on home-based businesses

"Russ Paley changed my life. I went from a 5-figure corporate-America engineering position to a lucrative 6-figure self-employed income. I own my own time now and I got back my freedom. You can, too, if you follow Russ's ideas."

—ANDREW COPPOLA, NJ